Insomnia

Howard Mahmood

FADE IN:
On credit sequence...

AN ARM
stretched out. Long, alabaster white. Beautiful. A WASH
CLOTH enters frame. Starts washing the arm with long, tender strokes.

A TUMBLE OF HAIR
thick and auburn. Being gently washed.

FINGERNAILS
being clipped with a shiny nail clipper. Short. Uniform.
Tidy.

EYEBROWS
brown with a touch of gold. A BRUSH comes into view.
Brushes against the eyebrow hair, then back again. Against.
Then back again.

PANTY-HOSE
pulled gingerly off a long leg. Folded neatly. The wash cloth begins between the toes.
Warm, soapy water.

HAIR
now dry. The HAND appears with a comb. Pulls down through the thick tresses.
It is only now that we see the hand is wearing a SURGICAL

GLOVE.
The gloved hand holds up the comb and pulls stray hairs from it. Places them in a big,
clear, plastic bag. In the bag we see the panty-hose, a folded flower dress, the nail
clippings.
Goes back to combing. Comes across a knot and yanks the comb through. The HEAD
rolls over to us. Her face is bruised, her eyes blank. She is lying on the floor.
Dead.
End of credit sequence.

INT. BUSH PLANE - THE KILBUCK MOUNTAINS, ALASKA - DAY
The loud THRUM of a bush plane. We CLOSE ON a small, cloudy window. Through
it we see an endless expanse of pine trees.

HAP (O.S.)
Jesus. Just look at all that.
PULL BACK to reveal HAP ECKHART and WILL DORMER sitting side by side.
Hap's at the window. Greying moustache, a little pudgy, wearing a brown suit. Holding
a folded over Seattle
Times.

2

HAP (cont'd)
I thought we had a population problem.
Everyone should just move up here.
(taps window)
Just look at it, Will.
Will's eyes remain on the file on his lap.

WILL
I don't need to look at it.
Will Dormer. Tall, handsome, expensively tailored suit.
Snakeskin cowboy boots. There's both a magnetism and a distance to him. An intense mixture. Hap glances at him.

HAP
Nothing wrong with smelling the roses.
Will looks up. We see the trace of a thick, ropy SCAR by his
Adam's apple. There's tension between him and Hap, just below the surface. He taps the file.

WILL
Tell that to her, partner.

ANGLE ON THE FILE
a stack of 8x10 PHOTOGRAPHS. Of the dead girl. Her eyes puffed up from bruises. The whites bloody. Contusions along her breasts and shoulders.

PILOT (O.S.)
Detective?
The PILOT's looking back at Will. Wearing a leather red baron hat.
PILOT (cont'd)
Better check your belts. We'll be landing in about fifteen minutes.
Will nods. The plane lurches. The file falls to the floor and the photographs scatter. The pilot catches a glimpse of them. Looks at Will.

EXT. BUSH PLANE - CONTINUOUS
The small yellow plane veers left. Clears a mountain top and gives view to the spectacular Alaskan coastline. The green of the Bering sea, the blanket of pine trees, the jagged rock of the beaches. Enormous.

EXT. LANDING STRIP - OUTSIDE NIGHTMUTE - DAY
A SIGN swinging in the wind: Nightmute, Alaska. Halibut
Fishing Capital of the World!
PULL BACK to reveal it hanging from the eave of a small, corrugated building. The "airport." Nothing else for miles around.
A mud-splattered Jeep Cherokee pulls up next to it. Brakes

3

SCREECHING. A YOUNG WOMAN hops out. About 23. Petite with short, brown hair.
Peers up at the sky. Brightens at the sight of the BUSH
PLANE coming in for landing. Smooths down her down vest.
Making sure the GOLD SHIELD on her belt's visible. Nervous.
Excited.

OLD MAN (O.S.)
Eleanor?
ELLIE BURR turns. Shields her eyes from the sun. An OLD MAN hosing down the side of the building.

ELLIE
Hey, Mr. Angstrom!

MR. ANGSTROM
What're you doing here?
Ellie puffs up.

ELLIE
Police business.

MR. ANGSTROM
Police business?
The old man screws up his face, confused.
MR. ANGSTROM (cont'd)
Didn't you used to baby-sit for us?

ELLIE
I don't babysit any more, Mr. Angstrom.
Just made detective three weeks ago.
A CAT jumps down off the roof. Angstrom sprays it.

MR. ANGSTROM
Boy, Charlie must be short-handed down at the station.
Ellie, used to not being taken seriously. Turns back to THE
ROAR of the bush plane as it taxis down the strip. Coming to a stop. She hurries over as the door swings open and...
WILL DORMER steps down. Slipping on his sunglasses.
Scanning the nothingness around him. Spots the swinging sign.

WILL
"Halibut fishing capital of the world."
Hap, right behind him. Rubs his neck.

HAP

4

This ought to be interesting.

ELLIE
(over the engine)
Detective Dormer!
They look down. Ellie reaches up and takes Will's bag. Then his hand. Shakes it vigorously.
ELLIE (cont'd)
It's a huge honor to meet you! Ellie
Burr. I'm here to take you to the station!
Will motions to Hap.

WILL
My partner...

ELLIE
Detective Eckhart! I know! Welcome to
Nightmute!
She leads them away from the plane. Takes Will's briefcase.

ELLIE
I just want to say how incredible it is to have you working with us, Detective
Dormer. I've followed all your cases.
Theodore Dineli, Frank and Casey
Prud'homme, the Port Angeles shootings...
Opens the back of the Jeep. Puts the bags inside.
ELLIE (cont'd)
...And especially the Leland Street
Murders. That was my case study at the
Academy.
The Pilot walks by. Taps her on the shoulder.

PILOT
Tell your dad the game's gonna start late this week, Ellie.

ELLIE
Sure thing, Spence.
She looks back at Will. Can't help but focus in on his scar.
Touches her own smooth neck. In awe.
ELLIE (cont'd)
That's where Ronald Langley cut you in the basement of his father's house on 325
Leland, isn't it?
Will smiles, taken aback by this girl's exuberance.

WILL
You did your homework, Officer.

ELLIE
Actually...
She throws a quick glance at Angstrom. Out of ear-shot.

ELLIE
I just made detective three weeks ago.

EXT. NIGHTMUTE POLICE DEPARTMENT - DAY
The Cherokee parked next to a police car outside a plain, one- storey building. The Nightmute Police Department. A totem pole stands out front.

CHIEF NYBACK (O.S.)
Will Dormer!

INT. CHIEF CHARLES NYBACK'S OFFICE - CONTINUOUS
Nightmute Police Chief CHARLES NYBACK gets up from behind his desk with a big smile. Ruddy, red hair sprinkled with grey,
Nyback wears a faded army sweater over his uniform.

CHIEF NYBACK
I'll be damned!
Limps from behind his desk and gives Will a shake and a slap on the back.

WILL
(warmly)
How you doing, Charlie?
Nyback shakes Hap's hand. A reunion.

HAP
Hey, Charlie.

CHIEF NYBACK
Christ. I haven't seen you boys since...

WILL
Just after Leland Street.

CHIEF NYBACK
What's that, then?

HAP
Eight years.

WILL
Seven years.

6

CHIEF NYBACK

Seven years? Where does it all go? That was some amazing time, though, wasn't it?

Looks at Will. Down at his boots.

CHIEF NYBACK (cont'd)

You haven't changed a bit, Will.

Will. Looks at Nyback's gut.

WILL

You have, Chief.

They LAUGH. Eyes twinkling.

CHIEF NYBACK

I knew that was coming. I deserve it.

He starts back over to his desk. Notices Ellie still standing by the door. Points to Will.

CHIEF NYBACK (cont'd)

Pay attention to this man, Ellie. He'll teach you how to be a great cop.

Ellie straightens. Smiles. Looks over at Will.

ELLIE

Yes, sir.

CHIEF NYBACK

That's all, for now.

Ellie, realises they want to be alone.

ELLIE

Oh. Right. Okay.

Backs out. Quietly closing the door behind her. Will unbuttons his jacket. Takes a seat.

WILL

Nice kid.

CHIEF NYBACK

(sits with a SIGH)

Got a love affair with police work.

Drives me crazy with it.

Will surveys the fishing poles leaning against the gun rack.

WILL

Keeping you busy up here, Charlie?

Hap picks up a cheap trophy. Reads the base.

HAP

"2nd prize Great Kodiak Salmon Catch."

CHIEF NYBACK

I told you seven years ago this was a stepping stone to retirement.
Nyback nods to Hap's Seattle Times. The headline: "Deeper
Investigation into Special Branch"...
CHIEF NYBACK (cont'd)
Looks like it's a good time for you to get up here, too. With all the bad business going
on down at Special Branch.
Will and Hap share a look. No more joking. Hap folds over the paper.
CHIEF NYBACK (cont'd)
Just five bad apples so far?

WILL
So far.

CHIEF NYBACK
What's the D.A. got them on?

WILL
Four unwarranted shootings, witness intimidation, and cocaine theft.
Nyback winces.

CHIEF NYBACK
How about you? How you faring?

HAP
They're all over us, Charlie.

WILL
They're all over everybody.

HAP
I.A.'s calling themselves the "Corruption
Task Force." Can you believe that?
Trying to root out any mistakes or
"oversights" any other Detectives may have made over the years. They're turning it into
a witch hunt. Something on the news about it practically every night.
Nyback pulls a stack of messages from his desk.

CHIEF NYBACK
Got a bunch of messages here from some guy named Warfield.
Hap tosses a glance over at Will.

WILL
That's I.A.'s pit bull.

CHIEF NYBACK
Wants me to keep him posted on all your movements up here.

Nyback turns and ceremoniously drops the messages into the trash.
CHIEF NYBACK (cont'd)
I'm just glad Buck could spare you a couple of weeks. Take you out of the frenzy. I gotta tell you, though, I sure don't miss big city police work. Not that I was ever a great detective. But up here there's no Bureaucracy. No
Public Relations. No blurred lines.
Just good guys and bad guys. Simple.
A cloud passes over his face.
CHIEF NYBACK (cont'd)
Except for this.
Holds up a file. The name written on the lip: KAY CONNELL.

INT. HALLWAY - MINUTES LATER
Nyback leads Will and Hap down a hallway. Crooked plaques and black-and-white pictures line the walls.

CHIEF NYBACK
Couldn't get a thing from the body. Not a trace. Town's never dealt with anything like this before.
They turn a corner and stop at a door. Will glances up:
MOOSE ANTLERS hanging over it.
CHIEF NYBACK (cont'd)
I've briefed everybody about your coming.
They know to follow your lead.
Nyback opens the door onto...

INT. BULLPEN - NIGHTMUTE PD - CONTINUOUS
...the bullpen of Nightmute PD. Wooden desks, a couple computers, a jumbled corkboard, an impressive gun cabinet. A RADIO's playing.
Three MEN look over. A young uniformed cop and two guys with heavy facial hair, Timberland boots, and flannel shirts. One of them's part Inuit. Ellie sits in the back. Reaches over to turn off the radio.
Will and Hap stand in the doorway. Sticking out like sore thumbs in their suits. Nyback jerks his thumb towards them.

CHIEF NYBACK
This is Detective Dormer and his partner
Detective Eckhart. On loan from Buck
Lundgard, Seattle Robbery and Homicide
Special Branch. They'll be helping with the Connell case.
The Inuit, FRED DUGGAR, snorts. Takes his feet of the desk.

FRED
Helping?

CHIEF NYBACK

9

(ignoring him)

Anything they need to see, you show them; anywhere they want to go, you take them.

(nods to Fred)

This is Detective Fred Duggar. He's been leading the investigation up to now.

Will puts out his hand.

WILL

Detective...

Fred tugs at his dark handlebar moustache. Stands.

FRED

Suppose you want to see the body.

EXT. NIGHTMUTE POLICE DEPARTMENT - DAY

Fred steps out of the station, pulls on a baseball cap.

FRED

We can walk from here.

He heads off across the parking lot. Will and Hap exchange a glance.

WILL

Guess that's what they call Alaskan hospitality.

ELLIE (O.S.)

Don't worry about him...

They turn. Ellie's come up behind them. Looks over at the hunched figure to Fred.

ELLIE (cont'd)

He's just mad 'cause you're taking over.

Fred stops up ahead. Sees her. Annoyed.

FRED

Ellie! Go type something!

INT. NIGHTMUTE MORGUE - LATER

CLOSE ON a faucet. A bead of water, quivering at the mouth.

Falls with a BLIP!

CORONER (O.S.)

Did a fundascopic examination and found papilledema and petechiae of the retina.

PULL BACK to reveal Will, Hap, and the COUNTY CORONER standing by a stainless steel table. The naked body of KAY

CONNELL is laid out before them. Fred hangs back.

The coroner tugs at her surgical gloves. She's in her late seventies.

CORONER (cont'd)

Clear cause of death was herniation of the brain stem due to intracerebral hemorrhage.

HAP

Beaten to death.

CORONER
Beaten to death.
Will points to the bruises on the body's shoulders and breasts.

WILL
What about these contusions?

CORONER
Superficial.

WILL
Any signs of rape?

CORONER
None.
The coroner starts to cover the body with a sheet.
CORONER (cont'd)
She was a nice girl. Played flute with my granddaughter.
Will stays her hand.

WILL
Wait.
He pulls the sheet back down. Studying the body of Kay
Connell. Starts walking slowly around the table. In his element. The faucet drips. Drips.
Drips.
He bends down to smell her hair.
WILL (cont'd)
He washed her hair.
Takes a handful and lets it fall from his fingers.
WILL (cont'd)
Combed it.
Continues around the table. Picks up one of her hands.
Examines her fingers, her nails.
WILL (cont'd)
Cleaned under her fingernails. Clipped them.
Continues down around her feet. Checks between her first and second toes.
WILL (cont'd)
Toes, too.
(to Fred)
You found nothing on the body?

FRED
No.
WILL

No fibers, skin flakes, hairs...

FRED
Like I said, no. We know about those things up here.
Will stands there. Looking down at the body. Slim. Young.
Beautiful. Skin like marble.

WILL
He knew exactly what we'd be looking for.
Made sure to cover up all his tracks.

HAP
Even the best make mistakes.
Will looks up and locks eyes with his partner.

INT. PIONEER LODGE - NIGHTMUTE - NIGHT
Will and Hap enter the lobby of the Pioneer Lodge. Big stone fireplace and heavy ceiling beams. MOOSE ANTLERS mounted above reception. They put their bags down by the desk. Look around.

RACHEL (O.S.)
Lower forty-eight.
They turn. RACHEL CLEMENT stands in a doorway behind the desk. Dunking a teabag into a mug. Long dark hair and intelligent eyes.

HAP
Lower forty-eight?

RACHEL
You're not from here. I can tell by your walk.

HAP
Oh? And how's that?

RACHEL
Unsure.
Hap smiles at her. Will checks his watch.

WILL
Detectives Will Dormer and Hap Eckhart.
There should be a reservation for us.
Rachel looks at him. Goes to a small file box on the desk.

RACHEL
(to Hap)
Your friend's all business.

WILL
I'm always all business.
He glances out the window. It's as bright as day.
WILL (cont'd)
Is it really 9:30?

RACHEL
(nods)
Alaskan summers. Hope you're an easy sleeper. It'll be like this all night.
She hands them two cards.
RACHEL (cont'd)
Sign here.

INT. WILL'S ROOM - NIGHT
Will's taken off his jacket and is unpacking. The room is sparse and creaky. Bed dips in the middle. He hangs a jacket in the armoire then returns to his suitcase. Pulls out his SMITH AND WESSON 45.
Lays it on the bedside table. Takes out a shoulder holster.
A back holster. A handful of shells. Lays them on the table. Then a small SMITH AND WESSON 39/13 9MM. Checks the magazine.
There's a KNOCK on the adjoining door.

HAP (O.S.)
Me.
Will SLAPS the magazine back.

WILL
Come on in.
Hap opens the door. A glimpse into his room: family PICTURES on his bedside table - a WOMAN and three teenage GIRLS.

HAP
See you have the same decor as my room.
He walks over to the big window. It overlooks the harbor.
Big, snow-capped mountains in the distance. One lone TUGBOAT in the harbor towing a freighter.
HAP (cont'd)
Same view, too.
(looks out)
I've been watching that tugboat for the last half hour. So small, pulling all that weight.
(beat)
We have to talk, Will.
Will reaches into his suitcase. Pulls out a shirt.

WILL

What do you want to talk about?

HAP
You know what about.
Will throws him a look.

WILL
We'll talk when we get back to Seattle.

HAP
When's that, a week? Two weeks?...
(heads over to him)
We have to figure out a plan of action now.

WILL
You know my plan of action.

HAP
To do nothing.

WILL
That's right.

HAP
Dammit, Will. Warfield had me locked up in his office again for five hours yesterday.
Five hours. Asking all kinds of questions...

WILL
He's asking everybody questions.

HAP
But he's zeroing in on me. On us.
Everyone's talking about it.

WILL
He's just rattling your cage.

HAP
Well, I gotta tell you. With a wife, three kids, and a pension plan in the balance, it's
rattling hard.

WILL
We say nothing. It goes away. Simple as that.
Will goes back to his suitcase. Hap follows. A thin film of sweat on his upper lip.

HAP

(lowers voice)
Look. We've tampered with evidence.
We've pushed witnesses. We've planted shit. And they're sniffing around like dogs.
Especially on the Dobbs case...
Will flares up. Struck a nerve. Turns to his partner.

WILL
Weston Dobbs killed an eight year-old boy and left him hanging in the basement like a
piece of meat. You remember that?

HAP
You know I remember that.

WILL
One word to I.A. and he walks.

HAP
Maybe not. We could talk to Buck...

WILL
No way.

HAP
Cut some kind of a deal. I heard that's what Flynn's doing...

WILL
Mike Flynn's a dirty cop, Hap! We are nothing like Mike Flynn. We did what we needed
to do to make sure that son-of- bitch Dobbs paid for what he did. And every bastard like
him. We say one word about it and every case we ever brought in is going to blow wide
open and they'll all walk. Every last one. And I am not going to let that happen. No
deals. No compromises. No discussions.
He grabs a hanger.

HAP
Goddammit, Will. You grab on to something and you don't let it go.
He takes out a handkerchief. Wipes his brow.

HAP
I don't know if it's because you think it's the right thing to do or because your pride
won't let you do anything else. I can't tell any more.
(steps back)
But I can tell you one thing. I'm getting too old for this cowboy cop stuff. Breaking the
rules. Cleaning up messes. We're a dying breed, Will.
You're a dying breed. I.A., the D.A., all those reporters - they don't care what you did
at Leland Street seven years ago. They don't care that you've made this your life. They
don't care about getting the bad guy...

Will turns on his partner, eyes burning.

WILL
I care.

The partners, lock eyes. Years of working together. A thousand things unsaid. Hap reaches for the door.

HAP (cont'd)
They're watching us, Will. Like it or not. They're watching us.

INT. WILL'S ROOM - NIGHT
Will's asleep. Kay Connell's folder open on his chest. It's dark in his room, quiet. Suddenly the shade on his window quivers and SNAPS up, flooding the room with light. Will's eyes pop open. He rolls over to look at the clock:
3:15. Squinting, he gets up and walks over to the window.
We can see the rest of his scar. Runs down deep across his sternum.
He yanks the shade back down. It bucks, then settles.
Satisfied, Will returns to bed. Plumps the pillow, pulls the blanket up around him. Closes his eyes.
The shade lurches halfway. Then SNAPS back up. Light pours in. Will's eyes open.

WILL
You got to be kidding me.

EXT. STREET - NIGHTMUTE - DAY
Will jogs along in a Sonics sweatshirt, a ring of sweat around his collar. He looks out over the harbor. Fishing boats coming in with their early morning haul. More halibut.
He checks his watch. Slows to a walk. Looks up and sees...
Ellie Burr standing on the front steps of the Pioneer Lodge.
Smiles. Holds up some car keys.

ELLIE
Fred wants us to meet him at the
Connell's.

INT./EXT. JEEP CHEROKEE - DAY
Ellie driving. A hula-girl, swinging from the rear-view mirror. Will in the passenger seat. Wearing a crisp suit.
Ellie hands him a take-out bag.

ELLIE
Brought you a bear claw. Just in case you were hungry.
Will takes the bag. Looks inside. Yikes.
ELLIE (cont'd)
Local delicacy.

WILL

Think I'll pass.

He puts the bag on the dash. Looks out the window.

Nightmute's main street. A line of shops. Undistinguished
Town Hall. Elementary school up on a hill. Sign out front:
Sign-ups for Midnight Little League!

WILL (cont'd)

What kind of calls you get around here?

ELLIE

Oh. You know. Small-time stuff.

Nothing like what you must get. Mostly drinking-related problems. Domestic abuse.
Barroom fights. Stuff like that.

She shifts down. Takes a steep turn.

ELLIE (cont'd)

In the summer months it's pretty quiet.

That's when there's work out on the boats. The rest of the year, though...

They pass a MAN walking along the road. Gnarled walking stick. Ellie calls out the
window.

ELLIE (cont'd)

Hey, there, Joe!

JOE waves. They pass.

ELLIE (cont'd)

That's Joe Willy. Took his family hostage in November. That was the most exciting
thing that happened last year.

I wasn't there, though.

(grinds gear)

Chief barely lets me handle anything above a misdemeanor.

Will looks over at her. Smiles.

WILL

Don't give misdemeanors a bad rap.

ELLIE

But they're so boring. All small stuff.

WILL

It's all about the small stuff. Small lies. Small mistakes. Small oversights.
People give themselves away in a traffic violation just as much as they do in a murder
case. It's human nature.

He looks over. Ellie's listening intently.

WILL (cont'd)

Aren't you going to write that down?

Ellie, searching her pockets for something to write with...

ELLIE

Let me just...

Stops. Looks over. Realises Will's teasing her.

EXT. CONNELL HOUSE - DAY
A small ranch house. Aluminum siding. FLOWERS piled up by the front door. TEDDY
BEARS. RIBBONS. Left by well-wishers.

MRS. CONNELL (O.S.)
I haven't tidied up, since Fred told me not to touch anything.

INT. HALLWAY - CONNELL HOUSE - CONTINUOUS
MRS. CONNELL, a big woman with a thick grey braid down her back, opens the door
to her daughter's room. Looks at Will.

MRS. CONNELL
I don't believe in keeping a child's room like a shrine.
Will heads into the room. Hap follows. A palpable uneasiness between them. Fred and
Ellie stand in the doorway. Mrs. Connell turns to go.

INT. KAY CONNELL'S ROOM - CONTINUOUS
A small bedroom. Pink shag carpeting and clouds painted on the ceiling. Pictures cut
from magazines pasted on the walls. A stack of tapes and a boom box in the corner.
Will stands in the middle of the room. Taking it in.

WILL
Typical seventeen year-old.
(beat)
She went to a party Friday night?

ELLIE
Down at a local dive the kids like to hang out in.
Fred throws Ellie a look. "Kids?" She's practically a kid herself. Will opens the top
drawer of the bureau. Roots beneath the panties.

WILL
No diary.
On top of the bureau, a stack of photos. A couple torn up.
Kay Connell and a GIRL with white-blonde hair. Laughing.

FRED
She left the party early. Friends said she had a fight with her boyfriend and stormed out.

WILL
What time was that?

FRED
Around twelve-thirty.

Hap picks up a bear on Kay's bed. A bell JINGLES when he shakes it. Will crosses to a closet in the corner.

WILL
Who was the last one to see her alive?

FRED
Randy Stetz. Her boyfriend. We've questioned him, searched his place.
Didn't find anything.
Will pulls a dress out of the closet. Small, black, elegant.
The tag's been cut out. He pulls out another, then another.
Feels the fabric.

WILL
These are designer. Expensive.
(looks up)
Could Randy Stetz afford these?
Fred and Ellie exchange a look.

ELLIE
He fixes boat engines.
Will looks around. Cheap wallpaper, torn window screens.

WILL
Well her mother didn't buy them for her.

HAP
What are we thinking?
Will reaches over to a heart-shaped box on the bedside table.
Pulls out a pretty gold necklace. Holds it up.

WILL
Kay Connell had an admirer.
He hands the dresses to Ellie. Heads out of the room.
WILL (cont'd)
I want to talk to the boyfriend.

INT. INTERROGATION ROOM - DAY
CLOSE ON a hand squeezing a shoulder. Hard.

WILL
You don't seem all that sad.
The shoulder jerks away. PULL BACK to reveal RANDY STETZ sitting at a wooden table in an interrogation room. Longish blond hair, wearing a Metallica t-shirt, trying like hell to grow a moustache.

19

RANDY

I haven't had a chance! You fuckers been all over my back since Monday!
He takes out a cigarette. It's bent. He lights it. Hap sits opposite.

HAP

You know smoking stunts your growth.
Randy throws him a look.

RANDY

Yeah, okay, fat-ass.

HAP

(smiles at Will)
More Alaskan hospitality.
Will goes over to a coffee machine. Pours a cup.

WILL

Did you love her?

RANDY

Huh?

WILL

Kay Connell. Did you love her?
Randy flicks his ash. Shrugs.

RANDY

Sure. She was nice.
Will turns with his coffee.

WILL

"She was nice." Wow. That makes me all soft inside. Ever occur to you she didn't love
you back?

RANDY

Huh?

WILL

You heard me that time.

RANDY

She loved me. She wanted to see me every night.

WILL

But she was seeing someone else on the side.
Randy glares.

RANDY

I don't know what you're fucking talking about.

WILL

Friday night, at the party - what'd you fight about?

RANDY

Stuff.

WILL

What kind of stuff?

RANDY

Just stuff. I don't fucking remember.

WILL

The other guy?

RANDY

I told you I don't remember.

WILL

After that she left the party to go to him.

RANDY

How should I know?...

WILL

Ran like hell to go to him...

RANDY

Fuck you, man! - I'm sick of all your fucking cop questions...
Will suddenly hurls his coffee cup and grabs Randy up by the collar. Nose to nose.

WILL

Now you listen to me, you little shit.
This fuck-the-world-Metallica-t-shirt crap may work with your mamma, but it doesn't work with me. You got mad at your girlfriend because she was seeing someone else. You want to be the last person who saw her alive or are you going to tell me who that is?
Randy's lip curls. Red-faced.

RANDY

I don't know.

WILL
You don't know.

RANDY
She didn't tell me.
Disgusted, Will shoves Randy back into his seat.

INT. HALLWAY - MINUTES LATER
Will walking out of the interrogation room. Ellie joins him.

ELLIE
He's a little surly, isn't he?
Will smooths back his hair. Checks his tie.

WILL
Just a little.
He reaches into his pocket and pulls out the gold necklace from Kay's room. Hands it to her.

WILL
I want you to check this out, Ellie.

ELLIE
We already did.

WILL
Do it again.

ELLIE
But there wasn't any...
Will stops. Ellie stops. Will puts a hand on her shoulder.

WILL
The small things - remember? The second you're about to dismiss something - look at it again.
Ellie smiles, teasing.

ELLIE
You want me to write that down?
Will, has to smile. She's quick. Looks down the hall. A bearded GUY on crutches. Ellie follows his gaze.

WILL
Who's that?

ELLIE

The bartender at Darrow's. He was there
Friday night.

WILL
Good. He's up next.
Will heads over to him. Ellie watches his neck. Her hand closing over the necklace.

INT. RESTAURANT - PIONEER LODGE - NIGHT
The Pioneer Lodge restaurant. Small, dark wood, a RADIO playing something between
Bluegrass and Folk. Some rough- looking GUYS at the bar. Throwing looks over at...
Will and Hap, sitting at a table. Studying faded menus.

WILL
(reading)
Halibut Calabrese. Halibut Olympia.
Halibut Cajun Style. Halibut fish and chips...
He puts down his menu. Reaches for his drink.
WILL (cont'd)
Can't wait to see what's for dessert.

HAP
At least there's variety.
Will drains his drink. Locks eyes with a big GUY over at the bar. Beer froth on his
moustache.

WILL
Looks like the natives are restless.

HAP
Will?
Will looks back at his partner. Hap's fidgeting with the end of his tie.
HAP (cont'd)
I think, I think I'm gonna talk to Buck when we get back to Seattle.
A cold flash down Will's spine.

HAP
I wish I could stick it out like you. I just, with Trish and the kids...

WILL
Don't do this, Hap...
Hap avoids his eyes.

HAP
I'm thinking I could get off with probation. Keep half my pension. That's all I want.

WILL

(hisses)
Goddammit, Hap. Think about what you're doing...

HAP
You don't have to be involved, Will.

WILL
You tell Buck and I'm involved whether I like it or not...

RACHEL (O.S.)
Ready to order?
The men look up, interrupted. Rachel is standing by the table with a pad. Hap tries to recover with a big smile.

HAP
Hey - you do everything around here?

RACHEL
Just about.
Will stands abruptly. Eyes on Hap. Trying not to explode.

WILL
I'll just have another Scotch in my room.
(turns to Rachel)
If you don't mind.
Just then, his cell phone RINGS.

INT. BULLPEN - NIGHTMUTE PD - NIGHT
Will bursts into the bullpen. Hap behind.

WILL
Where is it?
Ellie, Fred, and a couple other GUYS huddled around a desk.

ELLIE
Over here.
Will and Hap head over to them. One of the younger guys,
FARRELL, intimidated by Will's presence. Tucks his shirt into his dirty jeans.
They part to reveal a BLUE KNAPSACK laying on the desk. Mud spots all over it. An embroidered daisy. Will examines it.

WILL
We're sure it's hers?

FRED
Has her books in it.

HAP
What about prints?
Ellie shakes her head, unfortunately not. Will reaches into the bag. Pulls out two text books.

WILL
Biology and Algebra.
He shoves the books towards one of the guys.
WILL (cont'd)
Find out who she studied with.
He continues through the bag. Pulls out a little plastic bag with "Hello Kittys" all over it. Dumps out the contents.
WILL (cont'd)
Make-up.
Looks up at Fred.
WILL (cont'd)
Find out where she bought it.
Fred looks at him. Not happy with make-up duty. Will pulls out a hair brush. Hands it to Ellie.
WILL (cont'd)
Lab.
Next, a couple worn paperbacks.
WILL (cont'd)
(reading titles)
Otherwise Engaged, Murder at Sunset.
He looks up at the group.
WILL (cont'd)
Who here reads this kind of crap?
Farrell straightens.

FARRELL
I read that kind of crap.
Will tosses them to him.

WILL
Read them. Tell me anything that strikes you.
Down to the bottom of the bag. A Ziploc with a half-eaten sandwich and an apple core. Will hands them to Ellie.
WILL (cont'd)
Lab.
Upends the knapsack. Scraps, paper clips, gum wrappers.
WILL (cont'd)
That's it.
Fred reaches for the knapsack.

FRED
I'll stick it in the evidence locker...

WILL
No.
Will takes it, walks slowly over to the window. Thinking.
Twists the knapsack in his hands and looks out at the
TOTEM POLE standing tall outside. A black RAVEN alights on top of it. Pecks at the air. Turns. Seems to look right at
Will.
WILL (cont'd)
We put it back where we found it.
Will turns to them.
WILL (cont'd)
You said it was a fishing cabin.

FARRELL
Uh, right. About two miles outside of town.

ELLIE
On the beach.
Fred tightens his jaw.

FRED
Why are we taking it back?
Will ignores the question. Walks back towards them.

WILL
This murder was in the papers, right?

ELLIE
Yeah. All over.

WILL
Call all of them from here to Anchorage.
Tell them we now know that Kay Connell left the party with a dark blue knapsack, but we haven't recovered it yet.
(checks watch)
We can get it in by the morning editions.
He hands the bag to Farrell.
WILL (cont'd)
Fill this with random books. Make it look heavy.
Will pulls out a handkerchief. Wipes the mud off his hands.
Taking his time. Finally turns to Fred.
WILL (cont'd)
It'll eat this guy alive if he thinks he overlooked a detail.

EXT. ROCKY BEACH - OUTSIDE NIGHTMUTE - MORNING
POV through BINOCULARS
A WOODEN CABIN comes into focus. Right by the water. Hasn't been used in years. Weathered, slate roof. Algae growing up the sides.

HAP (O.S.)
Nice. Lighter than I remembered.
WILL lowers his binoculars. He's standing on the black rocky beach. It's damp, slick, and cold. A fog's rolling in.
Hap and Farrell are sitting behind a cluster of rocks. A couple paper bags and a megaphone. They're comparing guns.

FARRELL
Glock 40. All plastic save the barrel and firing pin. Never rusts. What do you carry down in Seattle?
Hap reaches into his holster. Pulls out a...

HAP
Smith and Wesson 45.

FARRELL
Excellent!
Fred Duggar's standing on the other side of them. He's got a pair of binoculars, too. They're staking out the cabin.
Been there a while.

ELLIE (O.S.)
Brought some coffee...
Ellie appears with a thermos. Crouching down. Fred turns, annoyed.

FRED
What are you doing here?

WILL
(answering for her)
I told her to come.
Fred shoots Will a look. Down at his cowboy boots. Will gives him a smile.

ELLIE
Anything yet?

WILL FRED
Nothing. Nothing.
Fred goes back to scanning, pissed.

FARRELL
Maybe this guy doesn't read the papers.

HAP
Or goes straight to the Sports Section.
Hap and Farrell chuckle. Hap unscrews the thermos. A cloud of steam.
HAP (cont'd)
Who gets first dibs?
(looks up at Will)
Will?
Will looks down at his partner. Holding out the thermos like a weird kind of truce. Will turns away, rejecting it. A swath of thick fog unfolds over the black rocks as...
Fred tenses.

FRED
(looking through binoculars)
I see someone!
Hap and Farrell scramble to their feet. Will whips up his binoculars.
POV THROUGH WILL'S BINOCULARS - a FIGURE making its way to the cabin. Furtive.

WILL (O.S.)
That's him.
Will lowers the binoculars. Snaps his fingers at the men.
WILL (cont'd)
Fan out.
Fred, Farrell and Hap. Start spreading out. Ellie steps up. Will looks back at her. Too dangerous.
WILL (cont'd)
Stay here, Ellie.

ELLIE
But...
Will puts up his hand. She stops short. He plunges ahead.
Hap. Will. Farrell. Fred. Fanning out. Silent. Keeping eye-contact. Will points to Farrell. Wants the megaphone.
Farrell, balancing on a rock, holds it out. Accidentally keys it. The feedback SQUAWKS. Fuck.

FRED
He's bolting!
POV THROUGH WILL'S BINOCULARS - the FIGURE, looking around, running towards the cabin. Leaping from rock to rock.
WILL reaches for his Smith and Wesson.

WILL

Go! Go! Go!

The men jump into action. Race down towards the cabin.

Fred and Farrell, nimble over the wet rocks. Will and Hap, harder going. Grab onto jagged edges, slip down small crevices. Rocks sticking out every which way. The fog, thick and white...

THE FIGURE disappears into the cabin.

FRED AND FARRELL leap up onto a tall boulder and jump down.

Run over to the door of the cabin, guns at the ready...

WILL rounds the boulder, Hap panting behind him. Joins Fred and Farrell at the door. Will levels his Smith and Wesson at the door, and with a nod to Fred as he KICKS it in...

INT. FISHING CABIN - CONTINUOUS

...the door CRACKS and swings in. The men rush inside.

WILL
Police!

They look around: Nothing. A few old nets, a wooden table rotted through. No knapsack.

In the corner, a TRAP DOOR, left open. Will races over.

Looks down into the darkness.

WILL (cont'd)
Goddammit!

Turns and points to Farrell.

WILL (cont'd)
You! Head back up to base...
(to Fred)
You! Go right and follow along the water...
(to Hap)
Hap! You go left...

The men nod.

WILL (cont'd)
Go!

They rush out the door and split directions. Will crouches down by the trap door and...

INT. TUNNEL - CONTINUOUS

...drops down into a dark, dank TUNNEL. Water dripping.

FOOTFALLS echoing. Will cocks his head. Left or right?

Starts sprinting down towards the lighter end of the tunnel, his own footsteps bouncing against the tunnel walls. He rounds a curve. Sound recedes...

EXT. TUNNEL - CONTINUOUS

...He exits the tunnel onto the rocky beach. Stops short.

FOG has enveloped everything - obscuring all vision, dulling all sound. Like a strange dream. Eerie.

Will blinks against the thick whiteness. Strains to hear any sound, anything. There's only the distant LAPPING of the water.

He tightens his grip on his gun and plunges into the fog.

Quick, careful steps. Stumbles over a rock. Waves his gun in defense. Eyes wide open like a blind man...

SUDDENLY a GUNSHOT. Off to the right. Will whips his head around.

EXT. UP ON THE BEACH - CONTINUOUS

Ellie, alone, jumps at the sound. Reaches for her weapon...

EXT. DOWN THE BEACH - CONTINUOUS

Will heads towards the sound. Reaching out for approaching rocks. Scrambles over a small bank and finds...

FARRELL rolled up into a fetal position on the ground.

Clutching his thigh. Blood seeping through his fingers. He looks up.

FARRELL
Sorry about...

WILL
Where is he?
Farrell can't answer that.
WILL (cont'd)
(impatient)
Where'd the shot come from?
Farrell lifts his bloody hand. Points off towards the water.

FARRELL
Over there.
Will disappears back into the fog, leaving Farrell behind.
Clambers back down towards the water, pausing every few seconds to listen, to adjust. Heart POUNDING. Blood pumping. Like an animal tracking its prey. Leaps up onto a plateau of rocks when...

SUDDENLY a DARK FIGURE flashes past him. The killer! Inches away. Will wheels around...

WILL
Freeze!
CRACK! Squeezes off a shot. Misses! Can't believe it.
Goes for another... Nothing! Jammed! The figure, disappearing. Will tosses his Smith and Wesson, reaches behind his back and whips out his SMITH 39/13...

EXT. UP ON THE BEACH - CONTINUOUS

Ellie, weapon drawn, making her way down the rocks. A HAND suddenly grabs her arm.

VOICE (O.S.)
Dammit, Ellie!...
Fred emerges from the fog.
FRED (cont'd)
Put that thing away! Farrell's down!...
CRACK! as another shot rips through the air. Fred and Ellie freeze.

EXT. DOWN BY THE WATER - MINUTES LATER
Fred and Ellie, skittering down the rocks. Getting closer to the water. Hear a voice ring out...

VOICE (O.S.)
Hap!
The fog starts to dissipate. They reach the water to see...

WILL DORMER kneeling beside the body of his partner. Lying in the water.
Shot in the stomach. Blood dribbling from his mouth. Will grabs him up by the collar.

WILL
Hap!
Starts shaking the limp body. Teeth clenched.
WILL (cont'd)
Hap!
Hap's head, rolls back. Mouth agape. Face white...
Will, rips off his tie. Presses it to the gaping wound... trying to stop the bleeding...warm blood, pumping into the water...
Ellie watches. Horrified. Fred races over to the body.
Feels for Hap's pulse.

FRED
Dormer...
Will, shaking Hap again. Jaw set. Eyes intense. Veins popping up along his temples.
Fred catches his shoulder.
FRED (cont'd)
Dormer! He's gone.
Will looks up at Fred. His face contorts.
Suddenly leaps to his feet. Grabs a rock and hurls it savagely into the thick fog.

INT. CHIEF CHARLES NYBACK'S OFFICE - NIGHT
Chief Nyback sits in his chair. Fingers interlaced. A somber expression on his face.

CHIEF NYBACK
And then you lost him.

Will sits opposite him. Wet, dishevelled, dirty. Hap's blood smeared all over his shirt.
Staring off into space.

WILL
And then I lost him. In the fog.

CHIEF NYBACK
About how long 'til you heard the suspect's second shot?
Will, hesitates.

WILL
Twenty, thirty seconds. I followed the sound down to the water. That's where...
He blinks. Looks down. Swallows.
WILL (cont'd)
That's where I found Hap.
Nyback sighs, shakes his head. Reaches down to his bottom drawer and pulls out a
bottle of bourbon and a glass.

CHIEF NYBACK
I think you need a glass of this.
He goes to unscrew the bottle, but Will shakes his head.
Stands. Paces. Rakes his hand through his hair.
Turns suddenly and swipes his arm across Nyback's desk.
Everything CRASHES to the floor.

WILL
(yells)
Why didn't I know about that goddamn tunnel, Charlie?
Nyback looks up at him. Calm.

CHIEF NYBACK
There's a bunch of those tunnels out there, Will. From bunkers over sixty years old. I
don't even know half of them myself, and I grew up here.
Will clenches his fists.

WILL
I had him, Charlie. Right in front of me. Not two feet. I could smell the son- of-a-bitch.
Playing with me. And I missed the shot. He was right there and
I missed the shot! Then my goddamned gun jammed...
Nyback gets up. Limps over to his old friend.

CHIEF NYBACK
Will, you can't blame yourself.

WILL
I had him!

CHIEF NYBACK
It's only gonna make you crazy.
Just then there's a soft KNOCK on the door. The men look over. Ellie sticks her head in. Speaks in a tone that belies that a man has recently died.

ELLIE
You wanted to see me?
Will turns his back to her. Nyback heads over.

CHIEF NYBACK
Right, Ellie.
Ellie flicks a look at the pile on the floor. At Will's back.
CHIEF NYBACK (cont'd)
I want you to take care of the investigation into Detective Eckhart's shooting.
Ellie looks at him. Confused. Lowers her voice.

ELLIE
But what about the Connell case? I'm on the Connell case.
Nyback puts a hand on her shoulder.

CHIEF NYBACK
We need paperwork, Ellie. You know that.
Just write up a quick report.
Ellie's shoulders droop. Thought she was playing with the big boys. Just then Will turns abruptly and grabs his coat.

WILL
I'm going to check on the roadblocks...
Nyback catches his arm.

CHIEF NYBACK
You're no good right now, Will. Go back to the Lodge. Try to get some rest.
Will looks at him. Know's he's right.

EXT. ROAD - NIGHTMUTE - DAY
CLOSE ON a SQUEALING tire, ripping around a curve...

INT./EXT. SILVER JEEP CHEROKEE - CONTINUOUS
Will driving. Speeding. Scenery whipping past the window.
His hands, tight around the steering wheel. The hula-girl, dancing beneath the rear view mirror, a smile plastered to her face.
He grows suddenly pale. Pulls the Cherokee off to the side.

EXT. STREET - CONTINUOUS

Will jumps out of the Cherokee, leaving the door open. Runs down an ALLEY behind a row of shops.

INT. ALLEY - CONTINUOUS

A couple industrial trash bins. Will leans his hand against the wall and vomits. Hovers for a moment, saliva dripping from his mouth. Braces himself. Heaves again. Hears a BUZZING behind him. Turns.

A DEAD DOG lying next to a dumpster. FLIES buzzing around its head. Teeth bared. Eyes wide open.

Like it's watching him.

INT. PIONEER LODGE - LATER

Will walks up to reception. No one there. Just wants his key. Rings the bell. In the back room, he hears a RADIO.

RADIO

...earlier this evening after an aborted attempt to apprehend a suspect. He was forty-five...

It clicks off abruptly. Rachel appears in the doorway.

Takes in the blood on Will's shirt.

RACHEL

I'm sorry about your partner.

Will looks at her. She walks over to the desk.

RACHEL (cont'd)

It's been on the radio for the last two hours. Nothing but that. Like when they found Kay Connell's body.

(sympathetic smile)

We're not used to this sort of thing up here.

She reaches for his key.

RACHEL (cont'd)

He was standing right there just a couple of days ago. Your partner. Exactly where you are now.

(beat)

I hope I was nice to him.

Will takes his key.

WILL

You were nice to him. He liked you.

He smiles faintly, turns to go. Just then the phone RINGS.

RACHEL

(answering)

Pioneer Lodge?...

(listens)

Hold on a second. He's right here.

Will stops. Turns. Rachel holds up the phone. Covering the mouthpiece.
RACHEL (cont'd)
John Warfield. He's called a couple of times.
Will's stomach drops. That's the last phone call in the world he wants to take. Rachel reads his face.
RACHEL (cont'd)
Want me to lie?
Will shakes his head. Steps back and takes the phone.
Clears his throat.

WILL
(into phone)
Dormer.
PAUSE. A bemused VOICE on the other end.

WARFIELD'S VOICE
Detective Dormer. I've been trying to reach you. I was very sorry to hear about your partner, Detective Eckhart.
It must have been a terrible shock, what happened this morning.
Will. Not giving this asshole an inch. Rachel, trying not to listen.

WILL
(into phone)
That's not exactly how I'd put it.
WARFIELD'S VOICE (cont'd)
No, no. I suppose not. But I look forward to reading the report. Very sad. Very sad. Funny...

WILL
(into phone)
What do you mean, "Funny?"

WARFIELD'S VOICE
Oh, nothing. Just that I felt Detective
Eckhart and I, Hap and I, were starting to make a real connection before you left. I sensed that he was ready to get some things off his chest. Did you sense anything like that, Detective? I mean, as his partner?...
Will, squeezing the phone cord with his bloody fist.
WARFIELD'S VOICE (cont'd)
...You were his partner for, what, about ten years?...
Will turns from Rachel. Eyes burning. Voice steady.

WILL
(into phone)
You know why everyone hates you,

Warfield? It's not your questions, it's not your press conferences, it's not even your cheap suits; everyone hates you

'cause day after day you suck the marrow out of real cops when you never had the balls to become one yourself. Well I got to tell you, it's a shame you're not up here with me because I'd love to show you right now just what a real cop is capable of. You just remember that when you're sitting at your bullshit desk reading your bullshit report on my dead partner!

SLAM! He hangs up the phone. Runs his hand through his hair. Turns back to Rachel.

WILL (cont'd)

Next time. Go ahead and lie.

EXT. ROCKY BEACH - OUTSIDE NIGHTMUTE - MORNING

Fog everywhere. Dense. White. Suffocating.

We're running through it. Clambering over rocks. Hearing the sound of our own BREATHING. Our own HEARTBEAT.

Adrenaline pumping. An animal tracking its prey...

SUDDENLY a DARK FIGURE flashes past. Just inches away. Playing with us. Taunting us. We whip round with our weapon and...

INT. WILL'S ROOM - LATE NIGHT

BANG! Will bolts upright in bed. A film of sweat over his body. Breathing hard. The sound that woke him: the window shade FLAPPING open. LIGHT floods the room.

Will gets up. Goes over to the shade and pulls it down. It lurches up halfway. He tugs it down again. It slaps all the way open. Will yanks it down so hard it rips off the window.

WILL

Goddammit!

He gets tangled in it.

WILL (cont'd)

Goddamned...thing!

Pulls it off and flings it in the corner.

INT. WILL'S ROOM - 4:22 A.M.

The digital clock flips to a new minute: 4:23. Will, pacing. Scratching at his stubble.

Unable to sleep. Keeps stepping on a SQUEAKY floorboard.

Slows near the ADJOINING DOOR that leads into Hap's room.

Hovers. Lightly pushes the door open. Sees...

THE PICTURES on the bedside table. A WOMAN and three teenage

GIRLS. Hap's family.

INT. BATHROOM - 5:18 A.M.

Water gushing out of the faucet. Will's WATCH sitting on the sink's edge. 5:18.

Will reaches up into the open medicine cabinet for a bottle of aspirin. Shakes out a couple. Cups his hand under the water and knocks the pills back.

Closes the medicine cabinet and CRIES out...

HAP'S REFLECTION looming behind him.

HAP
They're watching us, Will...
Will whirls around...

WILL
Hap!
...nothing. No one's there.

EXT. MAINSTREET - NIGHTMUTE - MORNING
CLOSE ON running shoes, POUNDING the tarmac. PULL BACK to reveal Will running down Nightmute's main street. Eyes bloodshot.
A COUPLE NATIVE ALASKANS walking into a hardware store. Stop talking and glance over at him.
A YOUNG MOTHER in her husband's work shirt. Lifts her small
KIDS into the cab of a 4x4. Watches him pass.
AN OLDER MAN fixing the broken "E" on his store front. Turns at the sound of Will's footfall.
Everyone edgy. Cautious. A murderer amongst them.
Will continues on. Looking straight ahead. Wipes the sweat from his neck. Slows to a stop just outside the...

LOCAL CONVENIENCE STORE
A blown-up picture of KAY CONNELL in the window. Below, a painted sign: We miss you, Kay.
A stack of newspapers by the front door. The "Nightmute
Ledger." The headline: Seattle Cop Killed by Suspect.
Will picks one up. Stares down at it. Rain starts to dot the paper.

CHIEF NYBACK (O.S.)
...We're going to bring down a couple of guys from Ridgemount, but I want us to step up the investigation here...

INT. BULLPEN - NIGHTMUTE PD - CONTINUOUS
Rain hammering against the windows. Chief Nyback addresses the bullpen. Everyone's there except Farrell.

CHIEF NYBACK
...Nightmute hasn't lost an officer in thirty-seven years, and even though
Detective Eckhart wasn't from here, he was as good as one of us on this case. I had the honor of working with him down in
Seattle for a number of years. He was a fine detective and an even better man.
Will stands nearby, watching the rain hit the windows. His suit pants are slightly wrinkled. Nyback nods towards Fred.

CHIEF NYBACK (cont'd)
Fred, you'll be working with Detective
Dormer directly from now on.
Fred, stroking his moustache, nods. Nyback turns to Will.
CHIEF NYBACK (cont'd)
Will? Anything you'd like to add?
Will looks up. Everyone's eyes turn to him. He shakes his head.

CHIEF NYBACK
Okay. Then let's get to it.
Feet shuffling. Chairs scraping the floor as people get up.
A sense of determination in the air. Will grabs his coat.

ELLIE (O.S.)
Detective Dormer?
He turns. Ellie is beside him, holding a map.
ELLIE (cont'd)
I'm sorry to bother you, but I was asked to write the report on...
(lowers eyes)
...you know what I was asked to write the report on...
(looks back up)
...Could you, just to be accurate, for the report, could you just point out where you were
when you saw Detective
Eckhart yesterday?
She holds out the map. It's of the small stretch of coastline. Red circles marking various
points.
Will looks down at her. Takes the map. Turns it around.

WILL
It's good to be accurate, Ellie. You're doing your job.
He looks down at the map. Ellie watching his face.

ELLIE
I'm so sorry about what happened. I know you did everything you could...
Will points to a spot. Cutting her off.

WILL
I was here.
Hands her back the map. Smiles. Just then Fred walks up.

FRED
Dormer. Still no sign of the bullet that went through Farrell.

WILL
I'm going to the hospital to talk to him now.
(looks at his watch)

You get the search party together. No fewer than thirty people. I'll meet you in exactly twenty-five minutes. Don't waste any time.

He pulls on his coat and heads for the door. Fred watches him leave. Sticks a toothpick in his mouth.

FRED
Partner or no partner. That guy's a prick.

ELLIE
He has to be a prick, Fred. He's a great detective.

INT. HOSPITAL ROOM - ST. FRANCIS HOSPITAL - DAY
CLOSE ON the cover of one of the paperbacks, Otherwise
Engaged by Walter Byrd.
PULL BACK to reveal Farrell lying in a hospital bed in striped pajamas, reading it. A tear runs down his cheek as he turns the page.
A SNICKERS BAR is tossed onto his lap. He looks up. Face brightens.

FARRELL
Detective Dormer!
Will stands by his bed. Farrell puts down the book. Picks up the Snickers.
FARRELL (cont'd)
You don't seem like the bring-an- underling-who's-in-the-hospital-a-Snickers-bar kind of guy.

WILL
I'm not.
He pulls up a chair. Nods to the paperback.
WILL (cont'd)
How's the book?
Farrell bites into the candy bar.

FARRELL
Oh, a real tear-jerker. Brody, the good guy, just got shot.
He stops chewing. Realises the association. Swallows uncomfortably.
FARRELL (cont'd)
Oh. I'm sorry. About Hap. Detective
Eckhart.

WILL
Thanks.

FARRELL
I wish I'd had the chance to get to know him better. Take him fishing or something.

WILL

39

He would have liked that.

FARRELL
We just gotta catch the bastard, right?

WILL
That's why I'm here. I need to know exactly what you saw yesterday, Farrell.

FARRELL
What I saw?

WILL
Anything. It's important.
Farrell takes another bite of the Snickers. Like a little boy. Furrows his brow, trying to remember.

FARRELL
Pretty much nothing. That fog was so thick. The bullet seemed to come out of nowhere. I don't even remember seeing any shapes. Then I saw you. But only when you came up close. Then you disappeared again.
(shrugs)
I guess I heard more than I saw.
Will sighs, rubs his eyes.
FARRELL (cont'd)
Sorry.

WILL
No. No. Don't be sorry. It's not your fault.
Just then a NURSE comes in with a Dixie cup. Pretty, freckled face. Not much older than Kay Connell.

NURSE
Time for your meds.
Farrell smiles at her, winks at Will.

FARRELL
Lonnie and I went to high school together.
Lonnie gives him the cup.

LONNIE
Just take the pills, Farrell.

WILL
How's the leg?

FARRELL

Oh, you know. Don't feel that much.
Bullet went right through.

WILL
Right. Got lost in the rocks.

FARRELL
We'll get the other one, though.
Will looks up. Farrell pops the rest of the Snickers in his mouth.
FARRELL (cont'd)
After the autopsy.

INT. HALLWAY - HOSPITAL - LATER
Will walks down the hallway. Light pouring in from a set of high windows. He looks tired. Set-upon.
POV of SOMEONE
WATCHING HIM. From a doorway. Not close, not far. A HAND comes into view. Small. Bruised knuckles. Holds on to the door jamb. Watches as...
Will suddenly stops. Skin prickling at the back of his neck.
Turns and looks around.
A MAN in a wheelchair.
A LITTLE GIRL tugging at her hospital gown.
A couple of NURSES laughing at check-in.
An empty doorway.
Nothing.

EXT. ROCKY BEACH - OUTSIDE NIGHTMUTE - MORNING
Back at the beach. We see nothing but fog. A VOICE comes through.

ELLIE (O.S.)
...and it was at this point that Detective
Dormer headed towards the noise...
Ellie emerges from the fog. Carrying the map and talking into a small tape recorder. She's climbing over the rocks, wearing a windbreaker a couple sizes too big.
A UNIFORMED OFFICER follows, carrying a camera. She turns to him.
ELLIE (cont'd)
Remember, Kepp, shoot everything...
(back to the tape recorder)
...wherein he discovered the wounded
Detective Farrell Brooks, having been shot in the vastus externus of the upper left thigh...
She climbs over the same bank Will Dormer climbed two evenings before. Finds...
ANOTHER UNIFORMED OFFICER, hanging out and smoking.
ELLIE (cont'd)
Francis!
He looks up. Pimples on his chin.

FRANCIS
What?

ELLIE
You're supposed to be Farrell. Shot in the thigh and writhing in pain.

FRANCIS
C'mon, Ellie. What's it matter?

ELLIE
Accuracy. That's what.
(points to the ground)
Now get down.
Francis looks up at her. Flicks his cigarette away and gets down amongst the rocks.
Holds his thigh like he was shot.

FRANCIS
Ow.
CLICK! Kepp takes the picture.

EXT. DOWN BY THE WATER - MINUTES LATER
Ellie sloshes through the water. Ankles getting cold.
Cheeks pink. But it doesn't matter. She's investigating.

ELLIE
(into tape recorder)
...shortly after hearing the second shot,
Detective Dormer continued through the water until he spotted the body, lying approximately fifteen feet away.
She stops. Looks at the map. At the spot Will pointed out.
Looks back up. Fog. Clicks off the recorder. Calls out.
ELLIE (cont'd)
You there, Rich?
A VOICE calls back. Someone pretending to be Hap.

VOICE (O.S.)
Yeah. And I'm freezing my nads off!
Ellie furrows her brow. Just then...
FRANCIS appears. Slips on a rock but catches his fall.

FRANCIS
Ellie! Think I found something!

EXT. ROAD NEAR BEACH - DAY

42

CLOSE ON a row of FEET. Mostly boots. Some more beat-up than others. Inching forward along a road.

WILL (O.S.)
...Anything catches your eye, you put it in a bag. Anything looks strange, you put it in a bag...
PULL BACK to reveal a long line of PEOPLE stretched out across the road about a mile up the beach. Some old, some young. Linking arms and moving forward. Looking down. The

SEARCH PARTY.
Will, walking up and down behind the line. Talking through a megaphone.
WILL (cont'd)
...Anything he may have dropped, moved, kicked, or stepped on, you put in a bag. Cigarette butts, gum wrappers, paper clips, coins, buttons - nine times out of ten a suspect leaves something behind...

VOICE (O.S.)
Detective?
Will turns. A couple burly GUYS with some BLOODHOUNDS.

BURLY GUY #1
Where do you want us?
Will points over to the woods on the other side of the road.

WILL
The woods. One group heading south, the other heading north.
Nods to Fred who's standing nearby. He hands the guys two radios.

FRED
Make sure they're set to channel 6...
Just then two young OFFICERS pull up in a squad car. Young and apple-cheeked. The first one holding a piece of paper.

OFFICER #1
We did the interviews with all the nearby houses like you asked.

WILL
Anything?

OFFICER #1
(shakes his head)
Here's a list of who we talked to.
Hands the list to Will. He glances it.

WILL

Alright. Go back and set up some follow- ups for this afternoon.
The Officers nod, put the car in reverse. Fred saunters over. Nods towards the searchers.

FRED
You don't think they should start further back?
Will shakes his head.

WILL
He had to have exited here. Over those boulders. I saw him move, he's nimble.
Would have taken the hardest way out.
Fred shrugs, skeptical. Just then, his cell phone BLEATS.
He reaches for it.

FRED
(into phone)
Duggar...
Will looks back at the search team. Slow. Meticulous.
FRED (cont'd)
(into phone)
Where was it?
A local WOMAN. At the end of the line. Glances over her shoulder. Looks at Will.
Smiles. You'll help us catch him.
FRED (cont'd)
(into phone)
Okay.
(slaps phone closed)
That was Ellie.
Will turns back to him.
FRED (cont'd)
They found Farrell's bullet. Says it looks like a 357. After the autopsy Rich can drive 'em both to the lab in
Anchorage. Have a murder weapon by morning.
Fred crosses his arms. Sarcastic.
FRED (cont'd)
That is, if it's alright with you.

EXT. PIONEER LODGE - NIGHTMUTE - NIGHT
Thunder RUMBLING.

INT. PIONEER LODGE - NIGHTMUTE - NIGHT
Rachel winding an old grandfather clock with a key. Looks about a hundred years old.
Will enters the lobby. Soaked through. Carrying an armload of wet files. Rachel turns,
sees him. Reaches over to an umbrella stand. Hands him an umbrella.

RACHEL
Here. It's on the house.

Will takes it. Preoccupied.

WILL
Thanks.
He starts up the stairs. Notices Rachel straining to return the key to the top of the clock.
Backtracks to help her.
She gets it without his help.

RACHEL
I got it.
(smiles)
Don't know why I bother. It's been broken for two years.

WILL
Habit.
Rachel looks at him. Can't figure this guy out. Remembers something.
RACHEL (cont'd)
Oh. A man came by to see you earlier.
Said he was your new partner.
A TINGLE skips down Will's spine. He looks at her.

WILL
Fred Duggar?

RACHEL
No. He didn't say what his name was.
Only that you were expecting him.

WILL
I'm not expecting anyone.

RACHEL
That's not what he thinks.

WILL
What did he look like?
Rachel thinks for a second. Leaning against the clock.

RACHEL
Short. Dark hair. Not that memorable.
Will nods, rubs his forehead. Suddenly has a pounding headache. Turns for the stairs.
Hesitates.

WILL
I need to borrow something.

INT. WILL'S ROOM - NIGHT

CLOSE ON a nail. One THWACK of a hammer and it bites into the wall. PULL BACK to reveal Will nailing the corner of a blanket to one side of the window. An ad hoc curtain.

He finishes that side. Starts to stretch the blanket across the window. Hesitates. Looks outside. To the left. To the right. To see if anybody's out there. If anybody's watching. Sees instead...

A LONE TUGBOAT chugging across the harbor. Pulling a huge freighter. Will squeezes his eyes shut. Opens them again.

Pulls the blanket fully across the window.

INT. WILL'S ROOM - 1:05 A.M.

The FILES spread across the floor. Their edges buckled from the rain. Dozens of pictures of Kay Connell. School records. Private letters. Health files. Coroner's report. Will. Pacing. Back and forth. Thinking. Over that same
SQUEAKY floorboard. The clock reads: 1:05.

INT. WILL'S ROOM - 2:20 A.M.

Will lying in bed. On top of the blanket. Wide awake.
Staring at the ADJOINING DOOR. Into Hap's room.

EXT. PIONEER LODGE - NIGHTMUTE - LATE NIGHT

Will, in a sweatshirt and coat, heads down the front steps of the Pioneer Lodge. Jams his hands in his pockets. The walk of an insomniac.

EXT. MAINSTREET - NIGHTMUTE - LATE NIGHT

Will walking down main street. In the middle of the road.

The dead of night. No cars. The sky a blinding white.

Hears some rowdy NOISE coming from a corner bar, beer lights flickering. A WOMAN rides by on a bicycle. Birds SINGING.

Not day. Not night. Stuck somewhere in between. Like a dream.

Turns down a side street. Passing more stores. Guns and
Ammo. Patty's Hair and Nails. General Store. Comes upon

THE ALLEY where he vomited the day before. Stops. Sees the DEAD DOG, still down at the end. Half obscured by the dumpster.

Will wavers, pale. Suddenly...

A HOMELESS MAN emerges from the shadows. Big. Wild-eyed.

Awakened from his sleep. Will, quickly backtracks to the sidewalk. Spooked.

JUST THEN the CRACK! of bat hitting ball. He turns. In the distance. Nightmute Elementary School.

EXT. NIGHTMUTE ELEMENTARY - LATE NIGHT

A Little League game in full swing. The uniforms, a little faded. The diamond, a little unkempt. A smattering of
SPECTATORS. Mostly dads with six-packs.

Will wanders over to the fence. Spots Ellie sitting alone on the bottom bleacher.

CUT TO:
POV OF SOMEONE
WATCHING HIM. From afar. The SOUNDS of the game, delayed a few seconds. Watches as Will crosses to the bleachers...

CUT BACK TO:
...and sits down next to Ellie. She turns, surprised.
ELLIE (cont'd)
Detective Dormer! What are you doing here?
(looks at watch)
It's two-thirty in the morning.
Shouldn't you be asleep?
Will glances out at the game.

WILL
I could say the same thing about you.

ELLIE
Oh. We always have play-offs in the middle of the night. It's the best time.

WILL
Who's playing?

ELLIE
The Puffins and the Hawks. We're in extra innings. The Hawks have a really good line-up this year.
She sips on a take-out coke. Looks back at the game. A plump, redheaded GIRL comes up to bat. Blows a bubble.

ELLIE
That's my sister.
Will looks over just in time to see the girl swing and miss by a mile. Ellie cups her hands around her mouth.
ELLIE (cont'd)
(calling out)
That's okay, Lib!
(to Will)
Usually she's better.

WILL
She your only sibling?

ELLIE
(nods)

Twelve years younger.

Libby takes another swing. Connects with the ball. Drops the bat and runs to first. Ellie gives a sharp WHISTLE.

ELLIE (cont'd)

What about you? You have any siblings?

WILL

No.

(rubs his eyes)

Well. I had a brother. He died when I was eleven.

Ellie, sits up...

ELLIE

Oh, I shouldn't have...

WILL

It's okay. Happened a long time ago. He was killed in a fire. In New Mexico.

ELLIE

That must have been awful for you.

Will leans back. Stretching his legs. Remembering.

WILL

Not really.

(slight smile)

I remember I was more embarrassed that he had died. Embarrassed that it made me different. So I didn't tell the other kids at school what had happened. They'd ask me where he was, where he'd gone. And I'd make up stories. He was visiting an aunt up north, he'd broken his leg, he was in a

Swiss boarding school. Stuff like that.

(shakes his head)

Nice kid, huh? Just kept making up more and more lies...

Suddenly, he stops talking. Slowly sits up. Sensing something. Ellie, noticing the shift.

ELLIE

You okay?

The row of DADS behind them. Jump up and start CHEERING.

CUT TO:

POV OF THE PERSON

WATCHING WILL. Sees him sit up. Look around. That same prickle at the back of his neck. A KID slides home just as...

CUT BACK TO:

...Will stands. Trying to shake the feeling.

WILL
I'm going back to the Lodge, Ellie.
Still need to go through some of Kay
Connell's school records.

ELLIE
(unsure)
Okay.
He turns to go, scanning the area. Ellie calls after him.
ELLIE (cont'd)
Try to get some sleep!

EXT. NIGHTMUTE MORGUE - EARLY MORNING
The Nightmute morgue. Next morning. A SQUAD CAR pulls up.
Francis gets out, whistling. Starts for the morgue's entrance.

INT./EXT. JEEP CHEROKEE - EARLY MORNING
Will in the Cherokee. Dark circles under his eyes. Suit jacket wrinkled. Pulls in next to
Francis' squad car.

WILL
(calls out window)
Officer!...
Francis turns.

WILL
I'll pick it up. You head back to the station.

INT. HALLWAY - NIGHTMUTE MORGUE - EARLY MORNING
Will walking down a hallway. Fluorescent lights.
Cinderblock walls. On his cell phone.

WILL
(into phone)
Duggar - I'm at the coroner's now. I'll be back in about twenty minutes...
Stops at an open doorway in time to see
THE CORONER pull a sheet over the cold, blue body of Hap
Eckhart.
Will's heart lurches. He grabs on to the door jamb. Wasn't ready for that. The coroner
looks up.

CORONER
Detective. Thought you were sending one of your lackeys.
Will clears his throat. Closes his cell phone.

WILL

I thought it was better if I came. Under the circumstances.
The coroner nods. Goes to wash her hands.

CORONER
It's different when you know them, isn't it?
(nods to clipboard)
Just sign over there and she's all yours.
Shrugs off her lab coat. She's wearing a blue dress. Looks like a piano teacher. Heads into an adjoining office.
Will. Alone. Steps into the room. The smell of formaldehyde. Bloody instruments on a stainless steel tray.
Walks towards the clipboard, eyes flicking over to the shape under the sheet when...
SUDDENLY Hap's HAND drops down. Thick fingers. Wedding band.
Will jumps...

CORONER (O.S.)
Your partner didn't suffer much...
The coroner re-emerges from the office with a manila envelope. Hap Eckhart written on it in black pen.
CORONER (cont'd)
Maybe for a minute or two.
Will rubs his face. Tries to focus on the clipboard. The coroner holds out the envelope. Smiles.
CORONER (cont'd)
Just enough time to reflect.

WILL
Thanks, Doc.
He takes the envelope. The coroner peers up at him.

CORONER
You're looking a little green, Detective.

INT. BULLPEN - NIGHTMUTE PD - DAY
Fred Duggar, dialing the phone at his cluttered desk.

WILL (O.S.)
So where's the other bullets?
He looks up. Will standing before him, holding the manila envelope.

INT. STORAGE ROOM - NIGHTMUTE PD - DAY
CLOSE on a key slipping into a padlock. Opens with a CLICK!
PULL BACK to reveal Fred and Will in a small storage room.
Standing in front of an army-green LOCKER. The evidence locker. Room's stuffed with old files and boxes. MOOSE
ANTLERS hanging over a small window. Will glances up.

WILL
What's with all the moose antlers around here?
Fred throws a look over his shoulder. Opens the locker.

FRED
Lots of moose.
INSIDE THE LOCKER - another manila envelope. The name on this one: Farrell Brooks.
Fred reaches back for the other envelope. Will, hesitant to give it to him. Feeling the bump of the bullet in the bottom corner. Hands it over. Wipes his brow.

WILL
When's Rich coming?
Fred slides it in beside Farrell's. Closes the locker door.

FRED
I'll call him now.

WILL
First I need a copy of the key.
Fred turns, a twinkle in his eye.

FRED
This isn't Seattle, Detective. We don't have copies.
(holds up key)
This is the only one.
Will looks at him. At the key. Plucks it from his hand.
Just then Nyback's SECRETARY appears in the doorway.

SECRETARY
Detective Dormer? Telephone.

INT. BULLPEN - NIGHTMUTE PD - DAY
The secretary hands Will the phone. Pulls something from under the desk. A beat-up BOX. Will's name on it.

SECRETARY
This came for you earlier.
Will glances at it. Takes the phone. Rubs his eyes.

WILL
(into phone)
Dormer.
Nothing. Someone's there but they're not saying anything.
Will, too tired for this shit...

WILL (cont'd)
Goddammit, Warfield, if you're gonna check up on me every...
Then...the VOICE. A MAN's voice. Not John Warfield's.
This voice is medium-ranged. Higher. Nose sounds stuffed.

MAN'S VOICE
I bet you haven't been getting much sleep.
Will straightens. Something weird.

WILL
(into phone)
What?
A little TITTER on the other end.

MAN'S VOICE
You lower-48s. You think the white nights are kind of neat. Then you can't sleep for
days. I've seen it happen about a million times. But you can't sleep for a different reason.

WILL
(into phone)
Who is this?
A PAUSE. Will loosens his tie.

WILL
(into phone)
I said, who is this?
The voice. Dropping to a WHISPER.

MAN'S VOICE
I saw what really happened, Will...
Will, furrows his brow.

MAN'S VOICE
I saw you kill your partner. With your back-up weapon. Out there on the beach.
I saw you shoot him dead...

CLOSE ON
Will Dormer's face.
As all the blood drains from it.
As all SOUND fades around him.
As his heart begins to POUND against his chest.
He falters, reaching out for the desk. To steady himself.
As if the floor's just dropped out beneath him. Eyes, darting around the bullpen...

WILL
(sotto, into phone)

Now you listen to me...

MAN'S VOICE
Don't worry. I won't tell anyone. Oh, and I saw you take my gun. My uncle's old 357. I dropped it in the rocks.
But you can go ahead and keep that.
CHIEF NYBACK, exits his office. Looks at Will and smiles.
MAN'S VOICE (cont'd)
...I mean...
(beat)
...Now that we're partners.
CLICK. The line goes dead.
Will, throat constricted. Listening to the DIAL TONE.
Smiles back at Nyback. Turns. Slowly hangs up the phone.
White as a sheet. Trying to act normal. Trying to act calm.
SOUND returning to the bullpen, like nothing's different.
Looks over at

THE BOX sitting on the edge of the secretary's desk. He reaches for it. Carefully, rips the packing tape. Bends back a flap.
Inside, some dark blue material. An embroidered daisy.
Kay Connell's knapsack.

EXT. NIGHTMUTE POLICE DEPARTMENT - DAY
Will, heading for the Cherokee. Clutching the box. Face pale, pace quick. Everything's different now.

ELLIE (O.S.)
Detective Dormer!
He closes his eyes. Now is not the time. Reaches the
Cherokee. Yanks open the driver's side door. Ellie catches up with him. Out of breath.

ELLIE
You look like you're in a hurry. I just wanted to ask you about these pictures.
She smiles, holds up some PHOTOGRAPHS. They're of the BEACH.
The ones Kepp took. Almost all fog.
ELLIE (cont'd)
I know they're not great quality, but this is where you said you were when you first saw Detective Eckhart, right?
Will. Barely glancing at them. Tosses the box into the car.

WILL
Right.
Gets in and closes the door. Puts his hand over the box.
Ellie comes up to the window.

ELLIE

But here's the thing. I retraced your exact steps according to your statement. You couldn't have seen Detective Eckhart from there. I mean, not in that fog.

WILL

Then change it.

ELLIE

How much closer would you say you were?

WILL

I don't remember.

ELLIE

Five feet? Seven feet?
Will, about to seriously lose his shit. Looks at Ellie.
Eyes dark, distant.

WILL

Listen, Ellie. I don't have time for this shit. Five feet, seven feet, twenty feet. Put down whatever you want in your report, alright?
He turns the ignition. Pulls out with a SQUEAL. Ellie steps back, watching him drive away. More curious than stung.

EXT. OUTSIDE NIGHTMUTE - DAY

The Cherokee. Parked off-road. A remote spot by the water.
The driver's side door, left open. The PING-PING-PING of the interior BELL.

EXT. BREAKFRONT - DAY

Will Dormer, walking along a breakfront. Aimless. One foot in front of the other. Staring out at nothing. The endless sea. Waves CRASHING. Wind HOWLING. Seagulls SCREECHING.
Everything. Closing in on him...
He stumbles over a rock. Grabs his head in his hands.
Stunned. Guilty. Ashamed. Fucked.
He saw it. He saw it!
A WAVE, explodes nearby. Drenching him in sea spray.
Will turns, raking his hand across his face. Blinking. Eyes stinging. Trying to focus. Trying to think this through...
Hears a dog BARKING in the distance.
Shakes his head. Looks at his watch.
Got to deal with the problem at hand.

INT. WILL'S ROOM - PIONEER LODGE - DAY

Will, bursts into his room at the Lodge. The shoulders of his coat still wet with sea spray. Crosses to the area of the floor where Kay Connell's files are still spread out.

Starts pressing the floorboards with the toe of his boot.

Testing. Testing. Until...he finds the one that SQUEAKS.

Gets down on his knees. Hesitates. Then jams his fingers in around the loose board.

Starts pulling it up. Face reddening. Knuckles whitening. Slips his hand into the gap.

Pulls out a muddy 357 RUGER.

The killer's gun.

Will, stares down at it.

INT. ALLEY - DAY

Will, standing at the mouth of the ALLEY. Just like the night before. Steps inside.

Cautious. Eyes darting.

Peering into the shadows for the HOMELESS MAN...

Not there. Coast's clear. Heads for the dumpster at the end of the alley. Shoves it aside.

Looks down at...

The DEAD DOG. Rancid. Rotting. Will gags. Holds a handkerchief to his face. Waving away the flies.

Then. Pulls the 357 Ruger from his pocket. Shrugs his coat off and wraps it around his hand and the gun. Looks away.

Fires a muffled SHOT into the dog's side. The body kicks.

Crouches down. Feels along the dog's ribs for the bullet's point of entry. Finds it. Pulls out a PENKNIFE and extends one of the blades. Cuts into the gash, fingers probing deep for the lodged bullet. He finds it. Pulls it out.

Looks back at the dog. Takes a deep breath. Wipes his brow.

A little smear of the dog's blood left on his forehead.

Turns and pulls a bottle of RUBBING ALCOHOL from his pocket.

Douses the bullet. Cleaning it. Glancing at his watch.

Running out of time...

EXT. NIGHTMUTE POLICE DEPARTMENT - DAY

The rear of the Nightmute PD building. Will, looking around, heads briskly for the back door...

INT. HALLWAY - NIGHTMUTE PD - DAY

...steps into the HALLWAY leading towards the bullpen. Hears

VOICES. Nearby. Ducks back. Waiting for them to fade.

Safe. Heads down towards the STORAGE ROOM. Glancing briefly at the PICTURES hanging on the wall. Of old time POLICE

OFFICERS. Striking brave poses...

INT. STORAGE ROOM - NIGHTMUTE PD - DAY

The storage room. Hot. Stifling. The moose antlers LOOMING over his shoulder. Will pulls the evidence locker key from his pocket. Unlocks the padlock. Swings the door open.

Pulls the Hap Eckhart envelope out. Throwing a look over his shoulder. Opens it. Shakes out the bullet that was lodged in Hap's spine. Then fishes a plastic bag from his pocket.

The bullet he shot into the dead dog. Drops that into the envelope and reseals it. Hands shaking.

Something. Catches the corner of his eye. He turns.

HIS REFLECTION in the locker mirror. The blood smear still on his forehead.

FRED (O.S.)
Dormer...

Will jumps. Quickly wipes the smear off and turns. Fred
Duggar standing behind him. RICH by his side. Will clears his throat, shoves Hap's envelope into Fred's hand. Then
Farrell's. Angry.

WILL
These should have gone out two hours ago.

SLAMS the locker door and brushes past him. Fred and Rich exchange a glance.

EXT. CEMETERY - NIGHTMUTE - DAY
CLOSE ON a YOUNG GIRL's face. Dark hair held up in two barrettes, wind tousling the curls. Reading from a piece of paper.

YOUNG GIRL
...And that's how I think Kay would want us to remember her...

PULL BACK to reveal Kay Connell's funeral. PEOPLE standing by the grave, most of them HIGH SCHOOLERS. The sky's a brilliant blue. Red fireweeds blanket the hillside.

YOUNG GIRL (cont'd)
...Swimming, reading, hiking through the
Kebaughs...

FRED, ELLIE AND WILL stand off to the side. Dressed in black. Fred looks like he's never worn a tie before. Ellie holds a potted plant. A gift for the bereaved.

YOUNG GIRL (cont'd)
...playing her flute, meeting at Darrow's after school...

Will. Eyes bloodshot. Not really listening. Not really paying attention. A thousand miles away. Tugs at his collar. Feels tight.

YOUNG GIRL
...And always, always with a smile on her face.

The young girl looks up. Folds the paper closed. People
SNIFFLE. Mrs. Connell, reaches out to squeeze her arm.
Some CHILDREN. Start circulating with plastic buckets.
Filled with white carnations. Handing them out.

VOICE (O.S.)
Want one?

Will, startled, looks down. A LITTLE GIRL stands before him.

56

Curly hair. Glasses. Holding up a bucket. He shakes his head. Looks back up at THE MOURNERS lining up to place the carnations on Kay's casket.

AN OLD MAN with a brass-tipped cane. Two GIRLS, look like sisters, holding each other up. A MAN with a thick red beard. A LITTLE BOY, about five, clutching a FLUTE tied with a pink ribbon...

Will, looks away. Then. At the end of the line. Something catches his eye.

RANDY STETZ in tight jeans and a down vest. In front of him stands a GIRL with white-blonde hair.

From the torn pictures in Kay Connell's room.

Will, straightens at the sight of her.

Sees Randy surreptitiously caress her ass.

EXT. CEMETERY - LATER

The service is over. People are heading back to their cars.

Fred yanks off his tie. Looks at Ellie.

FRED

We should go say hello to Mrs. Connell.

He starts off. Ellie, looks back at Will.

WILL

You go ahead. I'll be there in a second.

Ellie nods. Catches up to Fred. Will turns his attention back to RANDY AND THE GIRL. Over at the far end of the cemetery. Standing next to Randy's motorcycle.

EXT. AT THE EDGE OF THE FOREST - MINUTES LATER

Randy gets on his bike, strapping his helmet on. The girl's about to get on behind him.

WILL (O.S.)

Why don't I give her a ride?

They look over. WILL walking towards them. The wind whipping his jacket. His tie. Randy makes a face.

RANDY

Thought I smelled something.

WILL

Good to see you, too, Randy.

Will arrives at the bike. The girl, TANYA FRANCKE, looks at him curiously. Her long white-blonde hair, her skin almost translucent. Something sexy about her. Has the carnation stuck in the buttonhole of her jean jacket.

TANYA

Who're you?

EXT. GRAVESITE - CONTINUOUS
Fred shakes Mrs. Connell's hand. Ellie waits. Looks over and sees
WILL standing with Tanya and Randy.
Shifts the plant in her hands.

EXT. AT THE EDGE OF THE FOREST - CONTINUOUS
Will shows the gold shield on his belt.

RANDY
Fuckin' cop.
Randy kick starts the bike. It dies. He kicks it again.
Calls out over his shoulder.

RANDY
You coming or not?

INT. CHEROKEE - FOREST - DAY
Sunlight dappling through tall fir trees. Will drives.
Tanya sitting next to him. Her black skirt riding up.
Picking at the flaking polish on her nails.

TANYA
I never met anyone from Seattle before.

WILL
You're not missing much.

TANYA
What are you doing in this shit-hole town?
Will, shifts. Looks over.

WILL
You were good friends with Kay Connell, weren't you?
Tanya hesitates. Pulls a cigarette from her purse.

TANYA
I was her best friend.

WILL
Best friend?

TANYA
Since grade school.

WILL
That's a long time.

58

TANYA

We were like sisters. Knew everything about each other.

WILL

Must be tough for you. What happened.
Tanya shrugs. Lights the cigarette. Takes a drag.

TANYA

Everybody says I'm holding up great, considering. Don't even care if I go to school.
They're all worried I haven't cried yet.
She stretches. Her midriff showing. Shifts her body towards
Will.
TANYA (cont'd)
But there's no law against not crying, right?

WILL

What about Kay's other friends?
Tanya makes a face. Reaches out and taps the hula-girl.

TANYA

Do we have to talk about Kay? I don't want to talk about her right now. Let's just drive.
Go somewhere.
Will looks over at her. She blows out a plume of smoke.
Smiles. Seductive.

WILL

You want me to take you somewhere?

TANYA

Long as it's fun.
She reaches out a sinewy arm. Starts massaging the back of
Will's neck.
TANYA (cont'd)
Young, impressionable girl left alone with older, Seattle detective. Who knows what
we could get up to.
Will, impervious to the touch. Head, throbbing. Reaches for the gear. His foot, pressing
harder on the gas.

EXT. CHEROKEE - FOREST ROAD - CONTINUOUS
SCREECH! The Cherokee whips around a curve.

INT. CHEROKEE - CONTINUOUS
Tanya giggles. Likes the speed. Will, goes even faster.

EXT. CHEROKEE - CONTINUOUS

The Cherokee breaks free from the forest. Racing along a coastal road. Water CRASHING against the rocks.

Up ahead, a LOGGING TRUCK coming the other way. The Cherokee shifts lanes. Heading straight for the truck.

INT. CHEROKEE - CONTINUOUS
Tanya looks out at the truck. Still giggling.

WILL
How about this. You like this?
The truck BEEPS. Will goes faster. Tanya takes her hand from Will's neck. Holds on to her seat.

EXT. CHEROKEE - CONTINUOUS
The gap's closing fast. The truck BEEPS again.

INT. CHEROKEE - CONTINUOUS
Tanya looks over at Will. Not giggling any more.

TANYA
Hey...

WILL
Thought you wanted something fun...
Will goes even faster...

EXT. CHEROKEE - COASTAL ROAD
The truck and the Cherokee. On a collision course. The truck BEEPS wildly.

INT. CHEROKEE - CONTINUOUS
Tanya squirming in her seat. Not liking this any more.

TANYA
Move over!
Will staring dead ahead. Tensing his jaw. The TRUCK... bearing down on them...
Tanya reaches for the wheel...Will pushes her hands away...
The TRUCK...a breath away...
TANYA (cont'd)
(screaming)
Move over, you crazy fuck!

EXT. CHEROKEE - COASTAL ROAD
The truck and the Cherokee...just feet from each other...at the last moment...the Cherokee jerks out of the way...

EXT. ICICLE FISHING CANNERY - DAY

...SCREECHES to a stop near an old sign, Icicle Cannery. Gravel flying. Will gets out. Slams his door. Rounds the car and opens Tanya's door. She's screaming at him.

TANYA
You crazy son-of-a-bitch! You could have killed us!
Will reaches in and pulls her out of the car.
TANYA (cont'd)
Ow! You're hurting me!
Will pulls her up a steep hill of garbage and broken crates.
Pushes her down the other side. She stumbles.
TANYA (cont'd)
You want to tell me what the fuck this is all about?
Will stands above her, on the hill. His face set like stone.

WILL
You and Kay were like sisters?

TANYA
That's what I said.

WILL
Told each other everything.
(heads down the hill)
That why your picture's torn up in the top drawer of her bureau?
Tanya steps back.
WILL (cont'd)
Why her boyfriend's hand was clamped on your ass at her funeral?
He grabs her by the arm. Jerks it up. She CRIES out. Will leans in.
WILL (cont'd)
You like games, little girl? Well how about this one - you're standing right where her naked body was found wrapped up in a garbage bag.
Tanya's eyes grow wide. She looks around her. Disgusting, rotten. A SEAGULL pecking at the body of a dead bird. She tries to break away...

TANYA
No...

WILL
Who was Kay seeing besides Randy Stetz?
Tanya looks away.
WILL (cont'd)
Who gave her those dresses?
She struggles more. No good. Will's grip is like a vice.
WILL (cont'd)
I need a name.

TANYA
I don't know.

WILL
You don't know.

TANYA
She wouldn't tell me!

WILL
But you were such good friends...
Tanya, squirming. Angry.

TANYA
It was like some big fucking secret!

WILL
What was?

TANYA
She kept saying she was gonna get out of here. Leave us all behind. That he was going to take her!

WILL
Who?

TANYA
My arm!

WILL
Who?

TANYA
She used some stupid code name.

WILL
What was it?

TANYA
Brody...I don't know...
(crying)
...Something Brody!
Will straightens. He's heard that name before.
Suddenly Tanya jams her heel into his shoe. He CRIES out.

She breaks away from him. Runs up the hill. Turns. Tears streaking her face. Throws the carnation to the ground.
TANYA (cont'd)
You happy now, you fucking bastard?

INT. BOOKSTORE - NIGHTMUTE - DAY
CLOSE ON a FINGER. Running along a row of book spines.
Brundt...Buckley...Buss...Buckham...Byrie...
PULL BACK to reveal will in Nightmute's small bookstore.
Still in his funeral clothes.
In the "Mystery!" section. Not finding what he wants. Then, something catches his eye:
A BARGAIN BIN at the end of the aisle. Will limps down to it. Avoides eye-contact with a
YOUNG WOMAN shelving "New Arrivals!"
Reaches into the bin. Rummages through some paperbacks.
Then he finds it: Otherwise Engaged by Walter Byrd.
Underneath the title, he finds what he's looking for:
Another J. Brody Mystery. Flips to the inside of the cover.
A BLURRY PICTURE of Walter Byrd. Head turned to the side.
Walter Byrd was born in Watson Lake, Canada. He graduated...
Will's eyes skip down to the bottom:
Mr. Byrd currently lives in Umkumiut, Alaska, with his two labrador retrievers, Lucy and Desi.
Will looks up. Slaps the book closed.

INT./EXT. CHEROKEE - ROAD - DAY
Will drives, sipping take-out coffee. Trying to fight the stinging in his eyes. Passes a sign: Umkumiut, 30 miles.

EXT. TESORO ALASKA GAS STATION - UMKUMIUT - DAY
Will stands in a phone booth at the gas station. Flips through the phone book. His finger tracing down the "B"s.
Finds it: Walter Byrd, 451 S. Diamond Tooth, Apt. B.

EXT. DIAMOND TOOTH ROAD - UMKUMIUT - DAY
Sky's become overcast. Will stands across the street from a pale blue building. On the ground floor, a tackle store.
Above, looks like several apartment units.
He starts across.

INT. HALLWAY - APARTMENTS - DAY
Will heads down a narrow hallway. Tiled floor. Passes door
"A." Stops at the next one, "B." Knocks. Hears nothing but the muted tv from apartment "A." Pulls out his gloves.

INT. WALTER BYRD'S APARTMENT - DAY

With a CLICK the door swings open. Will, gloves on, pockets his credit card. Hears the CHING CHING of dog collars as

TWO LABRADOR RETRIEVERS stand at attention, GROWLING. Will's prepared.

Takes a bag of treats from his pocket.

WILL
Lucy. Desi.

The dogs break. Trot over to him. Wolf down the treats.

Will scans the place. Small, cheap. Matching sofa and easy chair, corduroy upholstery. The walls, lined with old 1950s movie posters. All second-rate detective movies: "Another

Shot in the Dark," "Lady Luck," "He wore a Black Hat."

Will walks across the room. Repulsed. The pathetic hovel of a killer. Looks into the

BEDROOM
Single bed. Books and magazines. A half-eaten tuna sandwich on the bedside table. "NYPD BLUE" calendar on the wall.

It's quiet. He walks over to a large DESK by the window.

Scattered papers. Computer. Mini cassette recorder.

On the wall, hundreds of newspaper articles. Some yellowing, some fresh. All about cops: "Officer Louis Saved My Life!"

"Shoot-out in Soho," "South Street Cop Takes Down Drug

Ring," "Seattle Cop Killed by Suspect..."

Will curls his lip. Starts looking through the papers on the desk. Underneath a stack, he finds an 8x10 PHOTOGRAPH. It's of Byrd, standing in front of a big, lakeside HOUSE. A RADIO

TOWER in the background. Walter Byrd's face is blurred, turned to the side. The photo from the book bio.

Will takes it. Starts roughly opening drawers. A box of animal crackers, a rubber band ball. Then, shoved in the back of the top drawer, an APPOINTMENT BOOK. Will flips through to today's date. Blank. Shoves the book into his pocket. Slams the door closed.

Then reaches back for his Smith 39/13. Checks the magazine.

Slaps it back in place. He's ready.

SUDDENLY the phone RINGS. A beige rotary on the desk.

Plugged into an ancient answering machine. It RINGS again.

The answering machine WHIRS. Then BEEPS.

WALTER'S VOICE
Now you're mad at me.

Will freezes.

WALTER'S VOICE (cont'd)
...I spotted your car around the corner.

You must have been in a hurry. Put some pieces together. Don't worry, I would have done the same thing...

Will turns back to the window. Looking furiously...

WALTER'S VOICE (cont'd)

Anyway...
(blows nose)
...I'm not coming home. So you shouldn't wait there all day. I mean, they'll wonder about you at the station.
You should be careful about following procedure, Will, especially now that...
Will lunges for the phone. Snatches it up just as CLICK! the tape cuts off.

WILL
Goddammit!
Enraged, he PUNCHES the receiver through the wall.

INT. HALLWAY - APARTMENTS - DAY
Will exits the apartment. Cradling his hand. Looks down at the tile floor. Scanning it for a broken tile. Finds one.
Bends down and plucks out a broken corner.
Places it carefully where the bottom of the door meets the door jamb. Just then. His BEEPER goes off.

INT. BULLPEN - NIGHTMUTE PD - DAY
Will strides into the bullpen. Wounded hand in pocket.
Ellie hunts and pecks at a typewriter. Glances up.
Fred, over in the corner. SLAMS a drawer in the filing cabinet. Turns.

FRED
Forget your pager?

WILL
What?

FRED
I beeped you over two hours ago.
Holds out a one-page report.
FRED (cont'd)
Got a fax from the lab. Murder weapon was a 357 Ruger.
Will takes the report. Heads over to the coffee machine.

WILL
Good.

FRED
And something else that might interest you.
He reaches into his desk drawer and pulls out a book. Holds it up. Otherwise Engaged.
In hardback.
FRED (cont'd)
Remember this?
Will blinks.

WILL
No.

FRED
One of the paperbacks we found in Kay
Connell's knapsack.
Will pours himself a cup of coffee. Trying to keep the stream steady. Ellie continues
typing...CLACK...CLACK...

WILL
That's right.

FRED
Mrs. Connell found this copy in the house.
(opens it up)
It's signed. Personally.

WILL
So?

FRED
This is a local writer. Kay had all his books. I think we should check it out.
CLACK...CLACK...CLACK...Will rubs his chin. Looks back at the report. Judicious.

WILL
I don't think it'll lead anywhere.
The CLACKING stops. SILENCE. Will turns around. Ellie's staring right at him - that
isn't like him.
He turns back to Fred. Beat.
WILL (cont'd)
Well. If he's local. Give him a call.
The CLACKING resumes.

INT. STAIRWAY - DIAMOND TOOTH ROAD - UMKUMIUT - LATE NIGHT
A dark stairway. Late at night. Will, bathed in shadows.
Climbs to the top. Quietly, carefully. He heads down a hallway. We recognise it. Back
where Walter Byrd lives.
Will approaches apartment "B." Slowly pulls out his weapon.
Cocks it. Waits a beat then swings out in front of the door.
Ready to fight. Ready to confront. Looks down...
Tile corner's still there.

INT./EXT. CHEROKEE - UMKUMIUT - NEXT DAY
CLOSE ON Walter Byrd's APPOINTMENT BOOK laying open.
Scrawled in pencil: 8:30. Dr. Agee.

PULL BACK to reveal Will sitting in the parked Cherokee. The appointment book on the passenger seat. Been there all night.

Insomnia. Taking its toll. His hair, no longer neatly combed. His face, pale and unshaven. His eyes, dragged open from fatigue. Looks like the whole world's pulling him down.

Staring down the street at a

BRICK BUILDING on the corner. A placard by the front door:

Dr. Florence Agee, D.D.S.

Will checks his watch. Rubs his eyes with the heels of his hands. Suddenly. Something tells him to look up.

A MAN in the distance, walking along the road. Towards Dr. Agee's.

He's in his forties. Short, shoulders sloped. Wears a beige, zip-up windbreaker, khakis, brown desert boots.

WALTER BYRD has a bulky hearing aid in one ear. Is looking down at the road. Glances up.

LOCKS EYES WITH WILL

Byrd, slows his pace.

Will, reaches for the door handle.

SUDDENLY

Byrd turns in the other direction, starts walking fast.

Will leaps out of the Cherokee and heads after him.

WALTER BYRD his short legs pumping, spots a TOUR BUS across the road.

Veers over to it.

WILL a runner's stride. Weaves through PEOPLE. Closing in on

Byrd. Sees his plan. Cuts across the road just as...

A PICK-UP rounds the corner. THUMP! Broadsides him. Will's pitched up and over the hood. Falls hard on the tarmac. Dazed for a second. Blood, gushing from his forehead. Hears the PICK-UP

DOOR open...FEET running over to him.

WOMAN'S VOICE (O.S.)

Are you alright? You popped out from nowhere!

More FEET running over.

MAN'S VOICE (O.S.)

He okay?

Will opens his eyes. Trying to focus. Looks up and sees, in the distance...WALTER BYRD getting on the tour bus.

Will struggles to his feet. The OLD LADY who hit him, wearing overalls. Reaches out.

OLD LADY
I don't think you should move.
Will stands, wavering. Flashes her his badge.

INT./EXT. PICK-UP
The old lady rips along in the truck. Will sits in the passenger seat, a handkerchief to his forehead. It's soaked with blood. The lady looks over.

OLD LADY
You sure you're okay?

WILL
I'm fine.

OLD LADY
Careful not to bleed on my interior.
Will looks over at her. Shifts in his seat. Ouch. Feels like a couple cracked ribs. Peers out the windshield at the
TOUR BUS a few cars ahead of them.

EXT. WINDY ROAD - CONTINUOUS
AERIAL VIEW of the pick-up tailing the tour bus. A windy coastal road. Beyond it, a blanket of endless evergreens.

EXT. FERRY STATION - OUTSIDE UMKUMIUT - DAY
A FERRY at the end of the pier. A small wooden booth for selling tickets. Beautiful, sweeping snow-capped mountains on the other side of the bay. Nothing else for miles around.
The pick-up pulls up next to the bus and a couple other cars.
Will jumps out. Scans the area for Byrd. Nothing. Then, sees the last few PEOPLE boarding the ferry.

INT. FERRY - MINUTES LATER
Ferry's getting pitched around in the roiling water. Most everyone is inside. TOURISTS with throw-away cameras, backpacks, anoraks, CHILDREN. Some looking sea-sick in the corner.
Will weaves through the crowd. Eyes darting, searching. The ferry lurches to one side, the crowd sways, Will spots
WALTER BYRD standing by a window.

INT. WINDOW - FERRY
Walter holds on to the railing. Looking at the view, the sea spray. Will comes up. Stands next to him. Cognizant of the people around them.

WILL

Walter Byrd.

Walter continues looking out the window. That same stuffed- nose voice.

WALTER

When I was seven my mother and grandmother took me to Vancouver. We were walking along the street one day when these two men ran past and snatched my grandmother's purse right from under her arm. Right from under her arm. That night a police officer came to our hotel room to ask us questions. Stood the whole time.

The ferry pitches again. Will grabs on to the railing.

Looking down at this little man. Hate in his eyes.

WALTER (cont'd)

His uniform looked brand new. His shoes and badge were polished, his billy club, his belt buckle. All perfect. He was like a soldier, but better.

Walter reaches up to blow his nose. Will's eyes look on in disgust - his knuckles are still red and swollen. From beating Kay Connell to death.

WALTER (cont'd)

Made a huge impression on me. His goodness. Gave me an instant respect for the police. I tried to become a cop when

I left high school, but...

He points to his hearing-aid.

WALTER (cont'd)

Congenital problem.

The ferry's engine HUMS to a stop. Walter smiles.

WALTER (cont'd)

Oh. We're here.

EXT. GENDREAU GLACIER - DAY

Gendreau Glacier. Spilling down between two huge mountains.

Enormous in its whiteness, its coldness, its silent power.

Will and Walter walk up its face, away from the other tourists. Walter leads the way. Hands in his pockets.

WALTER

You know this glacier moves a quarter of an inch every day?

He points off to the horizon.

WALTER (cont'd)

And on a clear day you can see all the way over to Newtok. There's a beautiful aviary over there. We can go sometime.

Will's lip curls. Watching him.

WALTER (cont'd)

It's actually cool for this time of year.

Normally the temperature runs about...

SUDDENLY Will lunges at him. Walter's eyes widen in surprise as he grabs him up by the collar. Nose to nose. Will barely keeping control.

WILL

69

You think this is a nice meeting we're having here? Friendly? Two people getting acquainted?
(jerks him harder)
You sick, coward, fuck. I get up every morning of my life just to bring someone like you down. Beating a seventeen year- old girl to death. Washing her afterwards, cleaning her. Make you feel like a real man?
(tightens his grip)
Huh?
Walter flounders.
WILL (cont'd)
I outta end this right now. Take a rock and smash your fucking skull in...
His jaws tense, nostrils flare. Walter, red-faced, sputtering...

WALTER
I stood right behind you...I saw you look right into his eyes and shoot him...
Will clenches his teeth.
WALTER (cont'd)
...Seattle's great hero. Shooting his own partner. I saw it all...

WILL
That was an accident! You hear me? I didn't know it was him!
(shakes him hard)
I didn't know it was him!
Just then a SHRIEK. Will looks over
A COUPLE KIDS. Further down the glacier. Having a snowball fight.
Will looks back at Walter. Has to take it easy. Shoves him away in disgust. Walter falls down onto the snow. Dislodges his hearing aid.
Watches Will pace. Head throbbing. Ribs, screaming in pain.

WALTER
Then why lie about it?
Walter brushes the snow off the dislodged hearing aid. Puts it back around his ear.
WALTER (cont'd)
I mean, I'm all for bending the truth.
That's what I do in my novels. It's my trade you might say. But why cover it up?
Gets up. Brushes the snow from his butt. Checks something in his pocket.
WALTER (cont'd)
You don't have to tell me if you don't want to. I'm sure you have some reason.
Something noble. I have faith in that.
Looks down at the kids. Shakes his head.
WALTER (cont'd)
They should be bundled up better.

WILL
What's your game, Byrd?
Walter turns back to him.

WALTER

No game.

WILL

The phone call. The knapsack.
Walter shrugs.

WALTER

I figured we're partners on this one. I mean, after what I saw...
Will stops short. Eyes burning. It's all he can do not to throttle this weed.

WILL

Let's get one thing straight, Byrd. We are partners on nothing.
Walter looks at him. Scratches his head.

WALTER

I research my novels. I know the procedures. You'd have cuffed me back at the ferry.
You'd have called for back- up, read me my rights, and gotten a search warrant for my
apartment. You're a well-respected detective. There's no reason for you to be talking to
me right now...
He takes out a handkerchief. Blows his nose.
WALTER (cont'd)
...except that we could help each other.
Will stares at him.
WALTER (cont'd)
So. We're at an impasse.
Will runs his hands through his hair. Half-crazed. Heart pounding. Turns to watch...
THE KIDS down the glacier. Making angels in the snow. Their
GIGGLES carried along by the wind.
Will, squeezes his eyes shut. Trapped. About to defy every instinct in his body.

WILL

(sotto)
You're going to get a phone call.
Walter steps up, tapping his hearing aid.

WALTER

I'm sorry?

WILL

I said you're going to get a phone call.

WALTER

(perks up)
Oh?

WILL
Kay Connell had a signed copy of one of your books.

WALTER
Thought you might find that.

WILL
You're going to be brought in for questioning.
Walter smiles. Pleased.

WALTER
Down at the station?

WILL
(hisses)
Yes down at the station.
Walter rubs his hands together. Thinking.

WALTER
Okay. Okay. Brought in for questioning.
Good. I can write this.
JUST THEN the ferry blows its HORN. Low and loud. Walter looks down at it.
WALTER (cont'd)
Ferry's leaving.
He starts down. Will watches him pass, has no choice but to follow. Walter, going over the details in his head.
WALTER (cont'd)
Something to divert...
Snaps his fingers. An idea.
WALTER (cont'd)
My gun. You still have my gun, right?
Will nods. Walter smiles. Spreads out his hands.
WALTER (cont'd)
Then that's the wild card. Every detective story has a wild card.

WILL
What do you mean, "wild card?"
TOURISTS. Boarding the ferry.

WALTER
Next ferry's in forty-five minutes.
Walter heads over to the ramp. Will stops, grabbing his side. A PANG through his ribs.
Excruciating. Calls out to
Walter.

WILL
What do you mean "wild card?"
Walter looks back. Waves.

WALTER
You'll know. At the questioning.
Gives his ticket to the TICKET TAKER. Gets on. Walks back to the stern. Looks out at Will. The HORN sounds again.
Walter, at the rail. Smiles. The ferry's engine, churning up water. Starting forward just as...
Walter takes a MINI CASSETTE RECORDER from his pocket. Holds it up for Will to see.
Will, on shore, sees it. A cold flash ripping through his body. That motherfucker. Bolts through some tourists towards the ramp but...
A couple of GUYS are just pulling it in. The Ticket Taker, grabs his arm.

TICKET TAKER
(to Will)
Full up.
Will, jerks his arm away. Stares off at the ferry. Walter
Byrd and his tape recorder. Receding into the distance.

INT. CONVENIENCE STORE - NIGHTMUTE - DAY
CLOSE ON a counter top. Stuff thrown down. Aspirin. Band- aids. Gauze. Medical tape. First aid cream. Back pills.
Sleeping pills. Bottle of scotch.
PULL BACK to reveal Will standing at the counter in the convenience store. His entire body aching. The CASHIER, throws him a look.

WILL
I have a cold.

EXT. CONVENIENCE STORE - MINUTES LATER
Will exits the store. A bag under his arm. We Miss You, Kay looming over his shoulder.
Steps out onto the sidewalk and sees...
ELLIE leaning against her truck. Waiting for him. Smiles.

ELLIE
Which way are you walking?
A tingle, all across Will's body. Christ. This girl's everywhere! He hunches into his coat. Flicks up his collar.
Doesn't want her to see him fully. Nods down the road.

WILL
Back to the Lodge.
Ellie grabs her bag. Joins him. They start walking.

ELLIE

I needed to get your signature on something.

She pulls a folder from her bag.

ELLIE (cont'd)

The report on Detective Eckhart. Chief made me finish it this morning. Said it was taking too long.

Will takes the file. Flips it open. The death of his partner. Neatly typed. Neatly stapled. Pulls out a pen.

ELLIE (cont'd)

Aren't you going to read it?

WILL

I trust you.

He signs. Hands it back to her. She slips it into her bag.

ELLIE (cont'd)

Now I can help you with the Connell case.

That writer's coming in tomorrow. Walter

Byrd.

A slight stutter in Will's step.

WILL

Duggar called him?

ELLIE

About an hour ago. Said he was more than happy to cooperate.

Ellie looks over at Will as they cross the street. Studying his face. His gait. Noticing the slight limp in his right leg. The cut on his forehead.

ELLIE (cont'd)

You haven't been sleeping much, have you,

Detective Dormer?

They arrive at the stone steps of the Pioneer Lodge.

WILL

Not really.

ELLIE

Isn't that the difference between a good cop and a bad cop? A good cop can't sleep 'cause a piece of the puzzle's missing. A bad cop can't sleep 'cause his conscience won't let him.

(smiles)

You said that once, remember?

Will, finally looks at her.

WILL

No. But it sounds like something I would've said.

Turns and starts up the steps.

WILL (cont'd)

See you tomorrow, Ellie.

Ellie, watches him for a second. Then calls out.

ELLIE

Oh! I forgot to tell you. The Puffins won.

Will stops, turns to look back at her. Confused.

ELLIE (cont'd)

The baseball game. Our team...

Slings the bag over her shoulder.

ELLIE (cont'd)

...We won.

INT. WILL'S ROOM - PIONEER LODGE - LATE NIGHT

Clock flicks to 3:00 A.M. Will, pacing in his room. Shirt off. Rib cage wrapped in a bandage. Looking through...

A STACK OF MESSAGES. All from John Warfield. He discards them one by one. Can barely focus...

SUDDENLY the phone RINGS. He lunges for it.

WILL

(grabbing it)

Listen to me, you son-of-a-bitch...

Interrupted by a CLICK...

RECORDED VOICE

...I saw you look right into his eyes and shoot him...

Walter Byrd's voice. Recorded from that afternoon.

RECORDED VOICE (cont'd)

...Seattle's great hero. Shooting his own partner. I saw it all...

Will, hears his own voice...

RECORDED VOICE (cont'd)

That was an accident!...

WILL

Goddammit, Byrd!

Then, another clumsy CLICK. Walter Byrd gets on.

WALTER

You'd have done the same thing, Will. I know you would...

He hangs up.

Will SLAMS down the receiver. Then again. And again. Yanks the cord out of the wall and HURLS the phone across the room.

EXT. ROCKY BEACH - OUTSIDE NIGHTMUTE - MORNING

...The DARK FIGURE. Disappearing back into the fog. Closing in around him like milky water...
We whip out our SMITH 39/13...plunge in after him...taking chase...BREATHING hard...leaping from rock to rock...the FOG, blanket thick...tightening around us...
Our feet. Hit water. Up to our ankles. Icy cold. We run...sloshing through...when...

SUDDENLY
A DARK FIGURE. Appears ahead. Big and hulking...CRASHING towards us...
We raise our weapon...quick as a flash...as the FIGURE emerges...
And in a split second...
WE LOCK EYES WITH FIGURE's - his eyes, brown and gentle...
CRACK! We fire! The FIGURE grips his gut, falls into the water.
Heart POUNDING. Adrenaline PUMPING. We slosh towards the body. Something...catching our eye...

A 357 RUGER lying in the rocks. Off to the side. We grab it. Turn back to the body...
And stop cold.
That's when it hits us. That's when we realize...

INT. WILL'S ROOM - LATE NIGHT
Will bolts up. White as a sheet.

WILL
I didn't know!
His body, drenched in sweat. His breathing, quick and ragged. Caught up in the twisted sheets of his bed. Looks across the room and sees

HAP sitting in the corner. Eating an apple with a penknife.

HAP
You sure about that, buddy?
He smiles. Sympathetic. Looks over at the window just as...
The BLANKET. Drops to the floor.
LIGHT floods the room.

INT. WILL'S ROOM - 4:02 A.M.
With a GRUNT Will puts his back into it. Shoving the heavy oak bureau towards the window. Sweat beading his face.
A...few...more...shoves. And the bureau finally stands in front of the window. WIll stands back to take a look. Only covers half of it.

WILL
Fuck!

INT. WILL'S ROOM - 4:35 A.M.
Red-faced, Will leans into the wooden armoire. Shimmying it towards the window...

CUT TO:
EXT. PIONEER LODGE - NIGHT
Ellie. Sitting in her truck. Parked behind the Pioneer
Lodge. Rubbbing her eyes. Sleepy. Looking up at

WILL'S WINDOW concerned.

CUT BACK TO:
INT. WILL'S ROOM - 4:35 A.M.
With one last heave, Will gets the armoire to the window.
Light still shining through the cracks.

INT. WILL'S ROOM - 4:50 A.M.
Will shoving magazines, blankets, sheets, pillows. Anything.
To fill the cracks. To cover the light. His eyes. Like a crazy man's...
SUDDENLY a knock on the door. Will turns.

RACHEL (O.S.)
Detective Dormer?

INT. HALLWAY - CONTINUOUS
Rachel standing out in the hallway. Will opens the door.

RACHEL
(startled by his appearance)
Will...I...

WILL
What is it?

RACHEL
There's a guy down the hall. Complaining about the noise.
(beat)
Says he can't sleep.
Will gives a half-smile. Fucking irony. Heads back into...

INT. WILL'S ROOM - CONTINUOUS
...his room. Rachel follows. Looks around at the mess.

RACHEL
Are you alright?
Will grabs up a sweater.

WILL
I'm fine.

He heads back over to the window. Rachel now notices all the stuff piled up. Softens her voice.

RACHEL
Did something happen?
Will. Cramming the sweater into a crack.

WILL
No.
Rachel walks up behind him. His cramming, more desperate.
More urgent.

RACHEL
Will...
He grabs a magazine.

WILL
The light. It keeps coming in...
Rachel reaches out. Catches his arm.

RACHEL
Will.
He stops. Looks down at her hand.
RACHEL (cont'd)
What happened?
Will suddenly realises what he's doing. Absurd. Pathetic.
Pitiful. Slowly turns to face Rachel.
Her eyes, looking up at him. His shoulders droop.
Exhausted. Rachel reaches up. Catches him in her arms.
Strong arms. Caring. Will buries his face in her neck.
Wants to be swallowed up.
Rachel holds him. Arms encircling. Will breathes her in.
Sweet, soft, safe.
Looks up. His mouth suddenly finding hers. A kiss, hungry, urgent. His arms move to surround her.

INT. WILL'S ROOM - LATER
Will and Rachel in bed. Spooning. Rachel behind will, her finger tracing his scar. Rain DRUMS against the window.
Will. Watching the raindrops streaming down the glass.
Casting strange shadows against the wall.

WILL
There was this guy named Weston Dobbs.
Twenty-four. Worked as a part-time stock boy in a copy store. Every morning he'd sit at the only window in his apartment and watch an eight year-old boy get picked up by

his carpool across the street. And every afternoon he'd watch the boy get dropped off again. He did this for about six months. Until one day he got up the nerve to cross the street and grab the boy before his carpool came.
Kept him in his apartment for three days.
Tortured him. Raped him. Made him do things...
Will tenses his jaw. Rachel, listens in horror.
WILL (cont'd)
When he was done, he got a rope and a kitchen stool and hanged the boy in the basement of the apartment building. But he didn't do a good enough job. The little boy's neck didn't break and he died from shock. The landlord found him five days later.
Rachel reaches for Will's hand. Squeezes it.

RACHEL
One of your cases?

WILL
Me and Hap. A year and a half ago. I knew the second I met Dobbs that he was guilty. Smug, cold. Dead eyes. We had circumstantial evidence, but nothing to tie him to it. Nothing concrete. Went over every inch of that apartment.
He pauses.

RACHEL
What happened?
Will turns slowly over to face her. Her hair, splayed out on the pillow. Her cheeks, flushed. Her eyes, listening.

WILL
We took some blood samples from the boy's body and planted them in his apartment.
(beat)
Arrested him the next day.
Rachel looks at him. Goose pimples on her arms. Realising the weight of the confession.

RACHEL
Will.

WILL
There've been other cases. Where we've changed results. Pushed witnesses. Manipulated evidence.
(rubs his face)
But Dobbs. I wanted Dobbs more than anything.
He sits up. Abrupt. Wincing from the pain in his ribs.
Rests his arms on his knees.

RACHEL
What if someone finds out?

WILL
We're under investigation now. Back in
Seattle.
(beat)
Hap wanted to talk. As soon as we got back. Thought he could work out some kind of deal.
Rachel rubs his shoulder.

RACHEL
Well, that's not going to happen now.
Will closes his eyes. The rain, PATTERING. Rhythmic.

WILL
Do you think it was wrong? What we did?
There's a PAUSE. Rachel, studying Will's back. The cuts.
The bruises. Not sure how to answer.

RACHEL
There are two kinds of people in Alaska.
Those who were born here and those who've come here to escape something in their lives.
(beat)
I wasn't born here, Will. I'm in no position to judge anyone. I'm not about that any more.
Looks out the window.
RACHEL (cont'd)
It's all about what you're willing to live with.

INT. WILL'S ROOM - MORNING
The clock reads 6:00. Will pulls on his trousers. Goes to strap on his Smith 39/13 holster. Grimaces with pain. Looks at his back in the full-length mirror. BLACK BRUISES seeping out from under his bandage.
Puts the 39/13 and holster in the top drawer of the bureau.
Turns and looks down at Rachel. Sleeping soundly.

FRED (O.S.)
You were acquainted with the deceased,
Kay Connell?

INT. INTERROGATION ROOM - CONTINUOUS
Will in the interrogation room. Standing by the window.
Tensed jaw.

WALTER (O.S.)
Yes I was.

WALTER BYRD sits at the table. Hair combed, wet. Shirt newly starched.

A Styrofoam cup of coffee in front of him. Playing the part.
Fred sits opposite him. Report file open. Ellie, next to
Fred. Taking notes. She's combed her hair, too.

FRED
In what manner?
Walter smiles modestly. Looks over at Ellie.

WALTER
She was, not quite a "fan." More an avid reader of my detective novels.

ELLIE
When did you first meet her?
Fred shoots Ellie a look. She closes her mouth.

WALTER
A year ago. At one of my signings.
Ellie hands Fred the hardback of Otherwise Engaged. He holds it up. Opened to the
signature.

FRED
Where you signed this?

WALTER
That's right.

FRED
What happened at that signing?

WALTER
She flattered me about my writing. Asked if she could visit me. To talk about my books.

FRED
Did she?

WALTER
Yes. Not that much at first. But then she became more comfortable. Started visiting me
every week...
Will, from over by the window. Interrupts.

WILL
What was the nature of your relationship?
Walter looks over. Wide-eyed.

WALTER
What do you mean, Detective Dormer?

Will turns. Accusatory.

WILL
She was an attractive girl. Did you have sex with her?
Walter blinks.

WALTER
She was only seventeen.

WILL
But she was an attractive girl.

WALTER
I suppose.

WILL
Did you have sex with her?
Fred shoots Will a look. Ellie, watching him.

WALTER
No.

WILL
But you wanted to.

WALTER
I was a mentor to her.
Will heads over to Walter's chair. Fists clenched in his pockets.

WILL
You gave her gifts.

WALTER
Yes.

WILL
Expensive dresses. A heart necklace.

WALTER
Yes.

WILL
Doesn't sound like a mentor to me.

WALTER
I gave her things she didn't have.

Couldn't have.
He turns to Fred and Ellie.
WALTER (cont'd)
Her family lives on Mr. Connell's disability. It isn't much.
Fred stops Will with a look. Had enough.

FRED
We understand, Mr. Byrd.
(to Will)
You want to sit down, Detective?
Tense BEAT. Will stares at Walter. Revulsion. Heads back over to the window.

WALTER
She wasn't happy. I was someone to talk to.

FRED
How do you mean?

WALTER
That boyfriend. Randy.
Fred, sits up.

FRED
Randy Stetz?

WALTER
That's right.

WILL
What about him?

WALTER
He. Well, he...
Walter hesitates. Takes a sip of coffee.
WALTER (cont'd)
I don't want to talk out of school. Kay told me things in the strictest of confidence. As
a friend.

FRED
Mr. Byrd. Anything you can tell us could help out with this case.
Walter furrows his brow. Taps his hearing aid.

WALTER
Well. He hit her.
Ellie's eyes widen. Fred glances at Will. But Will's too busy watching this little man
weave his web.

FRED
Are you sure about that?

WALTER
She'd come to me, sometimes in the middle of the night. Bruises all over her back, her upper arms. I pled with her to let me call the police, but she wouldn't hear it. Wanted to keep it a secret.

ELLIE
Randy Stetz beat Kay Connell?

FRED
(angry)
Ellie.
Walter looks right at her.

WALTER
He has a terrible rage. Kay even said he carried a handgun around with him.
Fred stands. This is big. Calls out the door.

FRED
Margaret! Get Judge Biggs on the phone!
(to Will)
I'll get another warrant for Stetz's place.
Walter takes a sip of his coffee. Cup's empty. Holds it out to Ellie. Smiles.

WALTER
Could I have some more coffee, Detective
Burr?
Ellie nods, takes the cup. Heads over to the coffee machine.
Fred turns back to the door...
AND AT THAT MOMENT Walter levels a look right at Will.
Mouths the words Wild Card.
A shiver down Will's spine. Wild card. The gun. Randy.

ELLIE over at the coffee machine. Pouring coffee. Glances up at the window. Catches the reflection of the two men.
An intense look between them.

EXT. ROCKY BEACH - OUTSIDE NIGHTMUTE - DAY
CLOSE ON a BOOT. Jumping down onto a black rock.
PULL BACK to reveal Ellie walking out on the beach. Heading down towards the water. Thinking.

INT. RANDY STETZ'S ROOM - NIGHTMUTE - DAY

84

A dark, narrow boarding room. A HAND reaches through an open window. Feels for the lock on the door. CLICK.

Will enters Randy Stetz's place. Cigarette butts, electric guitar, Hustler centerfolds tacked on the walls.

He looks around. Every inch of him revolting against what he's about to do.

EXT. ROCKY BEACH - CONTINUOUS

The sound of waves. A slight breeze. Ellie walking along the water.

Looking down. Brow furrowed. Stops and puts her hands on her hips.

INT. RANDY STETZ'S ROOM - CONTINUOUS

Will heads over to a hanging sheet on the other side of the room. Pulls it aside. A MOTORBIKE being repaired. Parts and tools all over the place.

Pulls the 357 Ruger from his pocket with a handkerchief.

Spots a COFFEE CAN on a shelf. Filled with thick oil.

EXT. ROCKY BEACH - CONTINUOUS

Something catches Ellie's eye. GLINTING from between the rocks. She bends down.

Pulls a pencil from her backpack.

Spears something and holds it up.

A SHELL CASING.
INT. RANDY STETZ'S ROOM - CONTINUOUS

Will, drops the 357 into the oil. Turns and heads back across the room. Hesitates. At the door. Turns back.

Looking at the oil can. Takes a step back towards it when he hears...

The sound of a SQUAD CAR. Pulling up outside.

Too late.

EXT. RANDY STETZ'S ROOM - LATER

Will stands just outside the doorway into Randy's room.

UNIFORMED OFFICERS inside searching the place. Tearing down pictures. Turning out doors. Ripping up carpet. Randy's voice. In protest.

RANDY (O.S.)
You can't fucking do this!

Will hears some SCUFFLING. The sheet being pulled down. The CLATTER of tools.

RANDY (O.S.)
Hey! I'm working on that!

Parts pulled off the shelves. The bike, shoved to the side.

Then. A SILENCE. Followed by...

OFFICER (O.S.)
Found something.

Will shuts his eyes. Heavy FOOTSTEPS head over to the bike.
Someone's pulled the gun from the can.

RANDY (O.S.)
What the fuck is that!
Fred's voice, calm.

FRED (O.S.)
That's it. Let's bag it.
More FOOTSTEPS. Randy, desperate.

RANDY (O.S.)
That's not mine, man! That's not mine!
Will opens his eyes. Fred's voice. Almost sympathetic.

FRED (O.S.)
Randy...

RANDY (O.S.)
No way, man!
More SCUFFLING. A chair knocked over. Something SMASHES.
Will looks down at the floor as
FRED AND A UNIFORMED COP struggle to drag Randy through the doorway. Randy
writhes, kicks, tugs. Screams.
RANDY (cont'd)
That ain't mine!
Fred grabs Randy's shoulder.

FRED
C'mon, Randy.
Randy squirms. Turns. Looks right into Will's eyes. Gone is the bluster. Gone is the
attitude. Randy Stetz, lost kid. Tears streaming down his face.

RANDY
I swear to God. I didn't kill her. I swear to God...

EXT. GARAGE APARTMENT - DAY
Will stands outside the garage apartment. Wind whipping his coat. Watches as a
Nightmute PD SQUAD CAR pulls off with
Randy Stetz in the back.
Fred sees him, heads over.

FRED
You look like shit, cowboy.
Will shifts his eyes to him.

WILL
That's an understatement.
Fred half-smiles. Watches the receding squad car.

FRED
Looks like we can wrap this one up.
Will barely nods. Fred pulls his baseball cap on.
FRED (cont'd)
We're getting together for a couple of beers later on. Might not be the Seattle thing to do. But you're welcome to come.
Fred puts out his hand to shake. Truce. Will looks at him.
Takes it.

INT. SHANTY BAR - NIGHTMUTE - NIGHT
CLOSE ON a tray of dark beer. Five glasses, foam sloshing.

FARRELL (O.S.)
I can't believe it. Randy Stetz.
PULL BACK to reveal Farrell, Rich, Francis, and Will sitting at a small, round table. Fred's passing out the beers. Dive bar. MUSIC blaring. 3 a.m. Happy Hour! banner on the wall.
Place packed with rough-looking FISHERMEN.
Rich takes a glass from Fred.

RICH
What do you mean, you can't believe it?

FRANCIS
He was an asshole.

FARRELL
That doesn't mean anything.
Fred sits. Takes a sip of his beer. To Farrell.

FRED
Didn't you grow up with him?
Farrell shifts in his seat.

FARRELL
Our dads were on the same boat.
(to Will)
We used to wait for them together.
Will nods. Jostled by the crowd. Reaches for his beer.

FRANCIS
He used to pick fights at the gas station.

RICH
And remember when he did all those donut holes that one summer?
He and Francis GUFFAW.

FRED
Just a bad seed.
Farrell looks over at Will.

FARRELL
How do you like our beer?
Will slams down his empty glass. Squeezes his eyes open and shut. Loud music.
Cigarette smoke.

WILL
I like it fine.
Fred pats Will's shoulder.

FRED
What Detective Dormer needs is a little shut-eye.

RICH
The white nights been hard on you?

WILL
They haven't been easy.
Francis grabs a handful of peanuts.

FRANCIS
They don't have titanium shades over at the Pioneer.

RICH
Well no wonder.

FRANCIS
You lose all sense of time.

FARRELL
Better than Fred's home town.
Will turns to Fred. Wiping the foam from his moustache.

FRED
My people are from Barrow. Way up north.

RICH
In the winter there's no sunlight for five straight months.

FRED
Like being swallowed up in a black hole.

JUST THEN.
ELLIE (O.S.)
Hi, guys.
They look up. Ellie standing by their table. Jeans, down vest. Hair tousled.

FRED
Nancy Drew! Pull up a seat!

FRANCIS
You hear what happened, Ellie?

ELLIE
Yeah.

RICH
Pretty cool.

FARRELL
Rich found the gun.

ELLIE
I know. I heard.
Fred leans back in his seat. Eyeballs Ellie.

FRED
Something's on Nancy's mind.
Ellie reaches into her vest pocket. Pulls out a Ziploc with the SHELL CASING inside.

ELLIE
I found this out on the beach.

FARRELL
What is it?

ELLIE
Shell casing. 9mm.
Will, blanches.

FRANCIS
Let it go, Ell. We got the bad guy.

ELLIE

None of us carries a 9mm duty weapon.
And the murder weapon was a 357.
Rich throws peanut shells at her.

RICH
Get a hobby, will ya?
Ellie brushes off the shells. Looks right at Will.

ELLIE
It's a legitimate point, isn't it,
Detective Dormer?
Everyone turns to Will. Their faces, spinning. He nods.

WILL
It's legitimate.

ELLIE
Worth pursuing?
He looks up. Holds her gaze. Then turns away. Grabs the side of the table.

WILL
The case is closed, Ellie.
(gets up)
I got the next round.
The guys don't protest. Will starts heading for the bar.
Weaving through broad shoulders, massive backs. Smoke.
MUSIC. Laughter. Arguing. A mass of bodies and sound.
Like being swallowed up in a black hole...
Looks back at the table.
Ellie, watching him.

EXT. ELLIE'S HOUSE - NIGHT
Ellie's truck pulls up in front of a small house. She jumps out.

INT. FRONT HALLWAY - HOUSE - NIGHT
SLAM! Ellie heads through the front door like a gust of wind. Thunders up the stairs.
Calls out.

ELLIE
Me, Pop!
We hear the TV in the other room. An older MAN, Ellie's father, appears in the doorway. Thick glasses, grey stubble, big paunch. Wearing a flannel robe.

ELLIE'S DAD
Ellie? You okay?
Ellie appears at the top of the stairs.

ELLIE
Where's all my academy stuff?

INT. BASEMENT
Pitch black, then, CLICK! as a bare lightbulb's switched on.
Ellie stands beneath it. Piles of crap everywhere.
She steps through the quagmire of old bikes, fans, auto parts. Over to a stack of cardboard BOXES in the corner.
She nudges through them, reading the writing on the tops. In thick black pen. Shoves a couple aside.
Then. Finds what she's looking for. Pulls down a box marked: Ellie Acad. Tears it open.
INSIDE - piles of papers, polaroids of her and her FRIENDS, schedules, syllabi, handbooks. Stuff from her Academy year.
At the bottom, a report. The title: "Securing the Crime
Scene," the Leland Street Murders. By Eleanor P. Burr.
Ellie pulls it out. Sits down on an old stool. Opens to the middle of the report. Her finger, tracing down the typewritten page. Flips to the next page. Then the next.
The next. Then. She spots it.
THREE-QUARTERS DOWN THE PAGE, her finger finds the sentence:...Detective Dormer's unregistered Smith and Wesson model 39/13 9mm, to immobilize Langley...
Ellie looks up. Chews her bottom lip.

EXT. MARINERS MEMORIAL - OUTSIDE NIGHTMUTE - DAY
CLOSE ON a huge wave CRASHING against a retaining wall.
Spray flying.
PULL BACK to reveal a small monument by the sea. A stone cupola with a bronze statue underneath. The sky, black with clouds.

INT. MARINER'S MEMORIAL - CONTINUOUS
Walter Byrd waits under the Mariner's Memorial. Wind whipping his jacket, the green sea churning behind him. Next to a fifteen-foot statue of a SEAMAN, tall, rugged, tough.
Holding on to a thick coil of rope.
Hunches against the wind. Watches as...
WILL approaches the monument. Sonics sweatshirt, wrinkled coat. Face drawn and haggard. Angry.

WALTER
(smiles)
Hi, Will...
Will enters the monument.

WILL
What the hell are you doing calling me at the station?
A gust of wind WHORLS through the monument.

WALTER
I figured we should touch base. Compare notes. I think it went well. What did you think?
Will's eyes pierce into him.

WILL
Randy Stetz is in jail.

WALTER
Told you I could write an ending.

WILL
Congratulations.
Will holds out his hand.
WILL (cont'd)
The tape.
Walter looks at the open hand. Hugs his jacket to him.

WALTER
I thought maybe we could talk some more.

WILL
There's nothing more to talk about.

WALTER
But we work so well together...
Will breaks. Rushes Walter. Slams him against one of the concrete pilasters.

WILL
We do nothing well together.
(SLAMS him again)
Nothing! You understand me?
Another wave CRASHES. Sprays them. Walter looks up into
Will's bloodshot eyes.

WALTER
You run on two settings, Will. I've noticed that...
Will tightens his grip.
WALTER (cont'd)
You jump from calm to rage in the blink of an eye. That's okay. I do that too.
He holds up the tape. Will grabs it, shoves Walter to the side. Yanks the tape out of the
cassette. Steps back and
HURLS it into the sea. Waves engulf it hungrily.
Walter watches him.
WALTER (cont'd)
You're not sleeping, are you?

WILL
What the hell do you know?

WALTER
Kay told me. She comes to me, you know.
Tells me things. About you. About me.

PAUSE.
WALTER (cont'd)
Does Detective Eckhart come to you?
Will curls his fists.
WALTER (cont'd)
Does he ask you why you shot him?
Whips around...

WILL
I told you that was an accident!

WALTER
Then so was mine...

WILL
Don't you pull that shit with me.

WALTER
I didn't want to kill her, Will.
Steps closer to him. Beseeching.
WALTER (cont'd)
When she called me that night from the party, she'd had a fight with Randy.
Wanted to talk. I told her to meet me at our special place. The cabin at the beach...
A couple RAVENS alight nearby. Flapping their wings.
SCREECHING into the wind.
WALTER (cont'd)
...When she came she was barefoot. And there was liquor on her breath. I only wanted
to comfort her. To touch her.
She could have at least let me do that.
Her skin...it was like everything I'd ever written about.
A dark shadow crosses his face. Holds on to the coiled rope of the statue. Will hisses.

WILL
Couldn't get it up, Walter?

WALTER
It was when I went to kiss her. She started laughing. I got angry. After all I'd given her.
All I'd shared with her. I just wanted to make her stop.

That's all.
Walter. Squeezing the bronze rope.
WALTER (cont'd)
From calm to rage in the blink of an eye.
Locks eyes with Will. Conspiratorial.
WALTER (cont'd)
Remember?
WILL'S HAND shoots out. Clamps around Walter's neck.

WILL
Like this?
Walter's face, starts turning red.

WALTER
Yes. Like that.

WILL
This an accident, Walter?

WALTER
If you want it to be...
Will looks deep into Walter's eyes. Squeezing harder. Pure hatred.

WILL
It took ten minutes to beat Kay Connell to death. Ten minutes.
Their eyes, locked. Veins, popping along Walter's temples.
Lip quivering...
JUST THEN a BELL sounds in the distance. Will looks up.
A LINE OF FISHING BOATS coming back in.
Will, looks back at Walter. Throws him to the ground.
Sickened.
WILL (cont'd)
Get the fuck out of town, Byrd. Leave and never come back.
Walter COUGHS. Holding his neck. Enjoying this.

WALTER
I have a summer house up by Kgun Lake.
I'm going to write my next novel there.
It's about a famous detective who goes bad.
Will shoots him a look.
WALTER (cont'd)
Just kidding.
He pulls himself to his feet. A little unsteady. Takes out a handkerchief. Dabs his forehead.
WALTER (cont'd)

94

The never coming back part, though. I'm not sure. To tell you the truth this has been kind of fun. Going to the station, meeting all those nice people. Talking with you.

He shrugs. Walks past Will.

WALTER (cont'd)

I might miss it.

Will turns. Watches him walk away. Walter hesitates. Turns back.

WALTER (cont'd)

I especially like that new detective.

Will looks at him. Back straightening.

WALTER (cont'd)

Detective Burr.

(smiles)

I liked her very much. Has a real vitality.

Will's stomach jumps. Walter turns back. Continues on.

The little man in a beige windbreaker.

INT. CHIEF CHARLES NYBACK'S OFFICE - NIGHTMUTE PD - DAY

CLOSE ON a HAND. Signing the bottom of a form.

CHIEF NYBACK (O.S.)

I was hoping not to send you back with so much paperwork, Will.

PULL BACK to reveal Chief Nyback sitting at his desk. Will stands before him. Signing papers. A bottle of bourbon on the desk. Some paper cups half filled.

CHIEF NYBACK (cont'd)

When are you taking off?

Will checks his watch.

WILL

Six-thirty.

Fred, standing over by the filing cabinet. Toothpick in his mouth.

FRED

If Spencer's not too drunk to fly.

Nyback chuckles.

CHIEF NYBACK

Can't talk you into staying for a couple of days? Do some fishing? Show you what normally goes on around here.

Will shakes his head.

WILL

I have to get back.

CHIEF NYBACK

Too bad...

Looks over at Fred picking his teeth.

95

CHIEF NYBACK (cont'd)
...Brought some real class to the place.
But, Seattle needs its hero back.
(stands)
Couldn't have done it without you, Will.
Will caps the pen. Uncomfortable. Nods towards Fred.

WILL
Had a lot of help from Nightmute's finest.
JUST THEN the door swings open. They look over as
ELLIE hurries in. She smiles. Looks tired.

ELLIE
Didn't want to miss anything.

CHIEF NYBACK
Detective Dormer's not leaving for a few hours.

ELLIE
Good.

CHIEF NYBACK
Maybe you could drive him to Spencer's.

ELLIE
Sure.
An awkward beat. Ellie walks over to Will. Looks up.
Suddenly throws her arms around him.
ELLIE (cont'd)
I thought what you did on this case was amazing.
Will holds his hands out. Not sure what to do. Looks down at the top of Ellie's head.

ELLIE'S HAND slips down his back. Feeling for a holster. For that 39/13.
Nothing. She breaks away.
ELLIE (cont'd)
We're really going to miss you around here.
She and Will lock eyes. Hold for a beat.
He knows exactly what she was trying to do.

INT./EXT. JEEP CHEROKEE - NIGHTMUTE - DAY
Will, driving down Nightmute's main street. He takes a left.
Goes up a hill. Glances out the window. Passing by
THE CEMETERY. A cluster of headstones. Something catches his eye. He stops the car.

EXT. CEMETERY - NIGHTMUTE - DAY

Will, walking up to the wrought-iron gate surrounding the cemetery. Stops. Puts his hands up to the bars.

KAY CONNELL'S GRAVE on the other side. Newly dug. A mound of dirt. Flowers, scattered by the wind. Daughter and Friend...1982-1999.
Will. Grips the bars. As if he's seeing it for the first time. Really seeing it.
Closes his eyes.
What have I done?

INT. WILL'S ROOM - PIONEER LODGE - EVENING
Will's REFLECTION in the mirror. He's showered. Hair's combed. Put on a clean suit.
Steps back. Smooths down his lapels. Just right.
Turns to face the room. Bed's made, mess cleaned up. He heads over to the bureau, pulls out his Smith 39/13. Lays it on the bed.
Unclips his badge from his belt. Lays it on the bed. Takes something from the bedside table. The BULLET found in Hap
Eckhart. Lays it on the bed.
All neat. All ordered.
Reaches under the mattress. Pulls out the PHOTOGRAPH of a blurry Walter Byrd standing in front of a house. A radio tower in the background. The call numbers: WKOZ.
Will studies it. Tears it in half.

INT. BACK ROOM - PIONEER LODGE - EVENING
Rachel in the back room behind reception. A pullman's kitchen, a desk, an old recliner.
Pouring some milk into a bowl for a CAT. A stray.
Will walks in. Rachel turns, smiles.

RACHEL
I found a new friend.
Will walks up to her. Puts his arms around her. Holds her, smells her, kisses her neck.
Pulls away. Looks into her eyes.
RACHEL (cont'd)
Will. What is it?
He doesn't answer. The cat, rubs against his leg. PURRING.

INT./EXT. JEEP CHEROKEE - EVENING
Will driving along a forest road. Eyes dead ahead. A map on the passenger seat. By the fold, Kgun Lake circled in pencil.

INT. BULLPEN - NIGHTMUTE PD - CONTINUOUS
Ellie working at her desk. Looks up at the clock: 6:00.
Gets up, grabs her down vest. Heads for the door. Farrell sticks the tip of his crutch in her path. She stumbles.

ELLIE

Very funny, Farrell...

EXT. ROAD TO KGUN LAKE - EVENING
AERIAL VIEW of the silver Jeep Cherokee. The only car on the road. The sky, white-grey. The trees, a blanket of green.
The Cherokee heads around a hairpin curve.

INT. LOBBY - PIONEER LODGE - EVENING
Rachel at reception. Reading the paper. Ellie walks in.

ELLIE
Hi, Rachel.

INT./EXT. JEEP CHEROKEE - ROAD TO KGUN LAKE - EVENING
Will, scanning the treeline. Takes a left fork then stops.
Thought he saw something. Grinds the gear, backs up. Takes another look.
IN THE DISTANCE, a radio tower. WKOZ.

INT. HALLWAY - OUTSIDE WILL'S ROOM - EVENING
Rachel and Ellie, standing outside Will's room. Ellie knocks again.

RACHEL
I would have seen if he came back.

INT. WILL'S ROOM - PIONEER LODGE - EVENING
The CLICK of a key and the door opens. Ellie strides in.

ELLIE
Detective Dormer?
She stops. Rachel behind her. Taking in the strange feeling in the room. Walks over to the bed. Eyes riveted on the
39/13. On the bullet. Rachel, behind her.

RACHEL
What is all this?
Ellie, her mind races. Notices TORN PHOTOGRAPH PIECES in the trash can. Reaches in and pulls some out. A puzzle.

INT./EXT. JEEP CHEROKEE - LAKE KGUN
Will stops the car at the end of a narrow dirt driveway.
Looming before him...
A HOUSE right on the lake. Tall, wooden, in disrepair.
Chipping yellow paint. A ghost of what it once was. The house from the photograph.

INT. STUDY - HOUSE
The CLANG of electric typewriter keys bang out a title:

BLINK OF AN EYE, by Walter By
WALTER BYRD hunched at his typewriter. In an old study.
Books stacked everywhere. Light patches on the walls where pictures used to hang.
BARKING outside. Walter cocks his head. Gets up. Walks over to the window.
OUTSIDE. Will walking up to the house. Lucy and Desi jumping around him.

INT. LIVING ROOM - SUMMER HOUSE
Will opens the screen door with a CREAK. Steps into the living room.
Recoils from the smell. Flies BUZZING. Yellow plastic covering the sofas. Boxes, books, papers, pictures piled high everywhere. Wallpaper faded, peeling.
Everything, decaying.

INT./EXT. ELLIE'S TRUCK - CONTINUOUS
Ellie ripping along the forest road in her truck. Gripping the wheel. The photograph pieces, taped together on the passenger seat.

INT. SUMMER HOUSE - CONTINUOUS
Will heads down a hallway. Dark, narrow, floorboards worn.
More shit stacked up.
Each step, careful, quiet. Tracking. Listening. A BREEZE sweeps through. The burned-out lightbulb hanging from the ceiling, starts swinging.

WALTER (O.S.)
Here to visit me?
Will whips around.
WALTER standing there. At the other end of the hallway.
Shoulders slumped.
Will shakes his head.

WILL
No.
FLIES, bouncing against the screen door.
WILL (cont'd)
I'm here to end this.
Walter looks around.

WALTER
Where's your back-up?

WILL
No back-up.

WALTER
You're not following procedure.

WILL

99

Procedure went out the window a long time ago.
Walter looks at him.

WALTER
We're on the same side, Will. You know that. After what we've been through together.
We're partners. Bound by a secret.
Will takes a step forward...

WILL
That's where you're wrong, Walter.
Slowly reaches into his jacket...
WILL (cont'd)
There is no secret. Because the biggest difference between you and me is what we will
or will not live with...
Pulls out his SMITH AND WESSON. Walter. Looks at the gun.
Inches back.

WALTER
Will...
SUDDENLY, darts out of sight. Swings back into the doorway with a SHOTGUN...
BAM! Will's shoulder explodes with blood.

EXT. DRIVEWAY - SUMMER HOUSE - CONTINUOUS
Ellie, jumping out of her truck. Hears the sound. Looks up at the big, yellow house.
Pulls out her Glock 40.

INT. HALLWAY - CONTINUOUS
Walter walking down the hall. Will, writhing on the floor, reaches for his back
holster...gun's not there!
Walter stands over him. Swings his leg back and...CRACK!
Kicks will in the ribs. The pain, blinding. Will GASPS.
CRACK! again, CRACK! again, CRACK! again. Walter's face.
Calm, flushed. A vein along his temple.
Will's eyes flutter. Blood, spewing from his lips. A THUD! to his kidneys. Walter stops,
out of breath. Hand on hip.

WALTER
You give the police a bad name, Will.
WILL'S HAND suddenly shoots out. Grabs the shotgun barrel.
WALTER stumbles back. The shotgun goes off. BAM! Chunks of ceiling rain down.
Walter falls to the ground.

EXT. SUMMER HOUSE - CONTINUOUS
Ellie, heart POUNDING. Kicks the front door open...

INT. HALLWAY - CONTINUOUS

Will, covered in dry wall, struggling to his feet. Reaches for his Smith and Wesson. WALTER'S DESERT BOOT kicks it out of the way. It SKITTERS down the hall. Walter grabs his shotgun. Scrambles to his feet. Runs down to the end of the hall. Ducks into...

INT. LIBRARY
...the library. Dirty shelves, strings of dust. Endless books. He races over to a cabinet. Yanks open a DRAWER...

INT. HALLWAY - CONTINUOUS
Will, on his feet, trying to focus. His suit, soaked with blood. Looking for his gun. Spots it, in the corner...

INT. LIBRARY
Walter jerks open another drawer. A STACK OF BOOKS teeter on the top of the cabinet. He finds what he needs. SHELLS.
Grabs a handful...
THE BOOKS tumble down on top of him. He CRIES out, covering his head...touches his ear, panics - hearing aid's gone!
Looks up. Will, coming down the hall...

INT. HALLWAY
Will hobbles into the library. Sweeps the room with this gun.
No Walter.
Steps on something, crushing it. Looks down. Walter's hearing aid. Kicks it aside.

INT. FRONT HALL - CONTINUOUS
Ellie. In the front hall. Following procedure. Right hand gripping the gun. Left supporting the butt.
Blinks away sweat. Facing three doorways.

INT. DINING ROOM
Will limps into the dining room. Furniture stacked high.
Eyes, darting. Gun, covering. Trying to stay conscious...
BANG! The screen door.

INT. FRONT HALL - CONTINUOUS
Ellie. Gun swinging. Doorway one. Doorway two. Doorway three...SUDDENLY

A FIGURE runs past number one. Big. Shadowy. The flash of a GUN.
She wheels toward it. Finger on the trigger...
SLO-MO...The FIGURE, passing. Her heart, POUNDING. Her finger...squeezing...
Will Dormer or Walter Byrd?
At the last second, she jerks the gun away. The figure disappears. She swallows. Gripping the gun. Follows.

EXT. BACK YARD - SUMMER HOUSE

The sky, heavy with clouds. The air, foreboding. Will steals out the screen door. Gun cocked. Eyes scanning.

Wind, bending the weeds, the trees.

BAM! a shot. Out of nowhere. Rips into his thigh. Will CRIES out. BAM! a second shot. Whizzes past him...

INT. LIVING ROOM - CONTINUOUS

...CRACK! the shot bites into the window frame. Wings Ellie halfway across the room. She drops to the floor. Clutching her shoulder. Flesh wound.

ELLIE
Shit!

Pulls herself over to a SIDEBOARD for cover. Shrinks behind it. Notices A PLASTIC BAG sticking out from one of the drawers. Nudges it open. A flowered dress, some panty-hose, strands of long dark hair...

EXT. BACK YARD - SUMMER HOUSE

Will. On the ground. Gripping his leg. Looking wildly around. No sign of Walter. Then. He sees it.

Lucy and Desi. Down by the boathouse.

INT. BOATHOUSE

The boathouse. Old, rotted wood. Crumbling beams.

Walter stands at a window. Re-loading his shotgun. He fumbles, drops a shell. It rolls towards a crack in the floor. Falls into the LAKE WATER below.

CLICK! Walter levels the shotgun out the window.

WALTER'S POV - the long, undulating WEEDS outside.

EXT. WEEDS

Will. Pulling himself through the weeds. Losing blood fast.

Dragging his body. Approaches the side of the BOATHOUSE.

WALTER'S GUN BARREL, sticking out.

Will ducks his head. Winces in pain. Breathing, becoming ragged. Rounds to the other side. Hoists himself up to another WINDOW. Cautiously looks in...

WALTER at the far window.

Will jerks back. Steps on the dock. A plank CREAKS. Shit.

Peers back through the window.

WALTER. Still looking out. Didn't hear a thing.

Will remembers. Walter doesn't have his hearing aid. He's deaf on that side.

INT. BOATHOUSE

Walter, looking out the window.

OVER HIS SHOULDER - we see Will climbing in through the window. Smearing blood along the sill, favoring his leg.

Stands straight. Levels his gun at Walter's back.

102

WILL
(softly)
Walter?
Nothing. Walter continues staring out the window. Will raises his voice.
WILL (cont'd)
Walter!
Walter jumps, whips around. Comes face to face with the barrel of Will Dormer's gun. Surprised. Absently touches his deaf ear.

WALTER
Wild card.

WILL
Drop the gun, Walter.
Walter looks at Will's 45.

WALTER
That jammed the last time, remember?
The men LOCK EYES. Wind HOWLING through the boathouse.
Killer and Detective. Only a bullet separating them.
WALTER suddenly jerks up his shotgun...
BANG! He stumbles back. Hit in the gut.
Will's Smith and Wesson, smoking. No longer jammed.
Walter, touches the blood. Looks back at Will. Staggering.
CRACK! The rotting floor gives way beneath him. He CRIES out, falls. Drops into the icy water below.
SILENCE. Will steps over to the hole. Looks down at
WALTER, floating on his back. Looking up at him. Water washing over his body. Eyes, pleading. Fading. A wave, gently pulls him away.

WILL
Another J. Brody mystery.

EXT. BOATHOUSE
Will staggers out on to the dock. Drops his gun. Crashes to his knees. Falls back. His face, pale. Lying against the wood of the dock.
RAIN DROPS. Start to fall. Washing the blood from his skin.
Puckering the lake water. Will's eyes...flutter...
FOOTSTEPS...running along the dock. Heavy boots...

ELLIE (O.S.)
Detective Dormer!
Will squints against the rain. Makes out the face of
ELLIE hovering over him. He gives a half-smile.

WILL

God, you're a pain in the ass.

Ellie kneels down next to him. Pulls over her vest. Covers him.

ELLIE

You're shot.

Will looks at her bloody shoulder.

WILL

You, too.

Ellie, tearing off her boot. Yanks off her sock.

ELLIE

I'm going to make a tourniquet.

Will, fading fast.

WILL

Walter Byrd killed Kay Connell. Her things are in the house.

ELLIE

I know.

WILL

Byrd's dead.

Ellie, wraps the sock around his leg. Starts twisting. Will grimaces. Ellie swallows. Doesn't want to ask this.

ELLIE

You shot Detective Eckhart, didn't you?

Will nods.

WILL

Yes.

A pained looks crosses Ellie's face.

ELLIE

Did you mean to?

Will shakes his head.

WILL

No. But I covered it up. I lied.

ELLIE

Why?

RAIN, drumming down around them. Will, takes a deep breath.

WILL

Because I just couldn't be wrong.

(looks at her)

Don't ever get that way, Ellie. Don't ever lose your way. It blurs the line.

His blood, pumping out in rivulets. Ellie looks down at him.

Her hero. Moves up to the wound in his arm.

ELLIE

This one looks worse.

Will reaches up a feeble hand. Stops her.

WILL

(whispers)

Just let me sleep, Ellie...

His eyelids, growing heavy.

WILL (cont'd)

Let me sleep.

Ellie blinks away the tears. Knows what he means. What he wants. Watches as the calm spreads over him.

Will closes his eyes.

ELLIE

No!

Will opens his eyes. She ties the second sock around his arm.

ELLIE (cont'd)

I will not let you sleep. If you've lost your way then you have to make it right.

That's the only way. That's what you'd tell me. I've been a detective for four weeks and I say you're coming with me.

She gets up. Slips her arms under his shoulders. Starts hoisting him up.

ELLIE (cont'd)

C'mon...

Will. Struggling to his knees. Every inch of him, screaming in pain. Gets to his feet. Arm slung around this tiny, young woman.

WILL

What about your shoulder?

ELLIE

Don't worry. I'll have a cool scar.

And they head, slowly but surely, back down the dock.

FADE OUT.

CPSIA information can be obtained
at www.ICGtesting.com
Printed in the USA
LVHW062205020322
712230LV00039B/1291